CONFIDENT PASTORAL LEADERSHIP

Original title: WHEN PASTORS WONDER HOW

CONFIDENT PASTORAL LEADERSHIP

HOWARD F. SUGDEN & WARREN W. WIERSBE

MOODY PRESS
CHICAGO

TO
Lucile Sugden
and
Betty Wiersbe,

who always have been a part of the
answer and not a part of the problem

© 1973

THE MOODY BIBLE INSTITUTE
OF CHICAGO

ISBN: 0-8024-1598-9

Second Printing, 1977

Printed in the United States of America

Contents

Contents

Preface

God has called us to be pastors and to preach His Word, and, quite frankly, *we enjoy it!* Phillips Brooks put it so beautifully in his first address in *Lectures On Preaching*: "Let us rejoice with one another that in a world where there are a great many good and happy things for men to do, God has given us the best and happiest, and made us preachers of His Truth."

It has been our privilege to pastor smaller churches and larger churches. At the present time, both of us are ministering in city churches. It has also been our privilege to minister in various conferences across the country. The most rewarding have often been the pastors' conferences where we have met with our brethren in the ministry and shared one another's burdens. Often we have conducted a question time when we have tried to encourage and enlighten the brethren from the Word and from our own experience.

The questions and answers in this book have grown out of these seminars. It has often been suggested to us that we publish answers to the questions that have been asked most frequently, and this explains the publication of the book you are now reading. These questions deal primarily with the pastor and his work in the church. This is not a book about theological problems or Bible questions.

We do not expect every pastor to agree with every answer we have given. But we do expect our brethren to consider each answer honestly and ask for God's direction. We have not sprinkled these pages with "I remember a case when" and "Now, this is what happened to me." Pastors are busy people who appreciate answers that are to the point. No doubt every pastor can write his own illustrations from his own experience!

Please keep in mind that we wrote out of our own experience and therefore cannot speak with authority about every local church. Our own ministry has been spent in churches with independent ministries, though in fellowship with others of like faith. We realize that different denominations have different ways of handling matters, particularly in the areas of church discipline and calling pastors. The brethren pastoring in these churches can still, we think, benefit from what we have to say.

We must confess that we had the younger pastor in mind as we wrote these pages. For some reason, many of them are not taught these basic principles in school; and if we can save them some trouble and trials, we will feel amply repaid for our efforts. But possibly the experienced pastor might be able to pick up a few new ideas or be reminded of some forgotten principle. The man who boasts that he has, say, fifteen years' experience in the ministry may not be telling the truth: perhaps he has had one year's experience — fifteen times.

At any rate, we send this book forth with the prayer that it will assist and encourage our brethren in the ministry, so that we might all be effective in winning the lost and building Christ's church.

HOWARD F. SUGDEN
South Baptist Church
Lansing, Michigan

WARREN W. WIERSBE
Moody Memorial Church
Chicago, Illinois

1

THE CALL TO THE MINISTRY

How can I determine whether I am called to the ministry, and how important is the assurance of a special call?

The work of the ministry is too demanding and difficult for a man to enter it without a sense of divine calling. Men enter and then leave the ministry usually because they lack a sense of divine urgency. Nothing less than a definite call from God could ever give a man success in the ministry.

How do we know we are called? For some, there is a crisis experience: Moses at the burning bush, or Isaiah in the temple. But for most there is simply that inescapable conviction that God has His hand upon us. Paul expresses it this way: "Necessity is laid upon me; yea, woe is unto me, if I preach not the gospel!" (1 Co 9:16). The man who is called has this inner conviction which will not permit him to invest his life in any other vocation.

Along with this there is the possession of the gifts and qualifications that God requires for His workmen. The candidate for the ministry had better pray over and ponder the words of Paul in 1 Timothy 3:1-7 and Titus 1:5-9. No minister feels adequately equipped; even Paul exclaimed, "And who is sufficient for these things?" But the man God calls senses that God has given him spiritual gifts and natural abilities which must be dedicated, cultivated, and used for God's glory.

9

Certainly the pastor must have character and conduct that are above reproach. He must sincerely desire to serve Christ. He should have a love for the Word and an appetite to study it and share it with others. He must be able to love people and work well with them. He must have spiritual and emotional maturity. If he is married, his wife should stand with him in his decision.

Along with this inner conviction, and an honest personal evaluation, must come an approval from those who know the Lord. This does not mean that we must "confer with flesh and blood," but it does mean that God's people will confirm what God has already said to the heart. If a man feels he is called to preach, he should begin to exercise his gifts in his local church and wherever God gives him opportunities. Spurgeon began his ministry by passing out tracts in tenement houses; D. L. Moody began as a Sunday school worker. It is wise to spend time with some seasoned saint (preferably your pastor) to discuss these matters and to seek God's guidance. It is significant that, in the Bible, God preferred to call people who were busy: Gideon was threshing wheat; Moses was tending sheep; David was with his father's flock; Peter and Andrew were fishing. It is difficult to steer a car that is in neutral, and God usually does not guide a believer who is "taking it easy."

Sometimes the church will sense God's call on a man's life even before the man senses it himself! John Knox was called to preach at the end of a sermon delivered by John Rough in St. Andrew's Castle, when the preacher charged him solemnly "to refuse not this holy vocation." Knox ran to his room, wept and prayed, and finally came out obedient to the call. George W. Truett had a similar experience when he was challenged to the ministry by an old deacon in a Baptist church in Whitewright, Texas. Truett said, "I was thrown into the stream, and just had to swim!"

A man does not enter the ministry because he has failed at

a dozen other jobs, or because there is nothing else to do. The oft-repeated counsel is worth repeating again: If you can stay out of the ministry, then do so; because this will prove you were not called to begin with. The man who is God-called will know it if he is sincerely yielded to God's will.

One word of warning: if you have unusual gifts but are not called to a full-time ministry, then get busy in your local church and use your gifts for God's glory; *but don't try to pastor the church.* The faithful, gifted layman who considers himself an "almost pastor" can either be a great help or a great hindrance in a local church. If he respects his pastor's divine call to be shepherd, he can be a great help. If he decides to "go it alone," he can create no end of trouble, particularly if he decides he is more gifted than the pastor God has called.

One final word of counsel: give yourself time to determine God's will. This does not mean endless excuses and delays! But it does mean spending extra time in prayer and in the reading of God's Word. Some of the greatest preachers determined God's leading while busy in other occupations. G. Campbell Morgan was a teacher in a boys' school and used his extra hours to preach and win souls. George Morrison served on the editorial staff of the great *Oxford Dictionary* while seeking God's leading for his life. When a man is quietly obedient in the everyday tasks of life, he will hear the voice of God and know which way to go.

Once I am sure of my divine call, what should I do next?

If you are not already exercising your spiritual gifts in a local church, then — *get busy!* 1 Timothy 3:6 warns, "Not a novice!" This suggests a time of spiritual maturing under the supervision of a pastor in a local church. Certainly if the deacon must "first be proved" (1 Ti 3:10), then the potential pastor ought also to have opportunity to prove himself.

God's usual plan is to let a man prove himself faithful over a few things before He makes him a ruler over many things (Mt 25:21). "Too much too soon" can lead to "too bad too late!" Spurgeon began as a Sunday school teacher. One Sunday he was asked to address the entire group because the leader was absent, and he was so successful that he eventually directed the school. Because Spurgeon was faithful to his little flock at Waterbeach, God gave him a great ministry in London. The man who is not faithful in the little tasks will never have opportunity to prove himself faithful in the big tasks. Start where you are; do what must be done; and let God open the way.

Perhaps the leaders of your church will want to license you to preach. A license to preach is to ordination what an engagement ring is to marriage: it's the first step, and it can always be revoked. Paul warns the church leaders, "Lay hands suddenly on no man" (1 Ti 5:22). Before the church lays hands on you for ordination, be sure God has laid His hand on you for a lifetime of service. It is better to be patient and certain than to be impetuous and embarrassed.

Start praying and planning toward specialized training. Your pastor and other mature Christians can give you guidance concerning available schools. Please don't use the old excuse that many great preachers never went to school! Spurgeon, Moody, Ironside, and G. Campbell Morgan never attended any schools for pastoral training; yet two of them founded schools for training preachers, and the other two sat on learned faculties. They knew the importance of education.

Watch out for the devil's attacks during this period. He often uses other Christians to discourage the would-be preacher, and sometimes even uses former pastors! Maintain a strong devotional life. Be devoted to Christ — be disciplined — be busy! Claim Proverbs 3:5-6 and Psalm 37:3-5.

What really is "adequate preparation" for the ministry?

God has many ways of preparing a man, and we should never despise or question His ways. He has a specific purpose for each of His workers, and He alone knows how to prepare His tools. Rule One: Keep your eyes on the Lord and not on other Christians — especially preachers!

There is more than one kind of preparation for the ministry. There is, for example, *general* preparation that comes from daily living. Paul was a tent maker; Peter and James and John were fishermen; and each of these men learned much about people and life just from their daily vocation. Many a practical lesson is learned in the office or factory, so never despise your hours of labor. Fortunate is the pastor who has punched a clock and has learned by experience what it means to be a Christian in today's workaday world!

Of course, there is *vocational* preparation as well: study of the Word, knowledge of Bible languages, an understanding of doctrine and church history, and practical training in the know-how of Christian service. "Apt to teach" is one of the important qualifications for the ministry, and this suggests "apt to learn." We must be receivers before we can be transmitters. The man who does not learn the discipline of study will never accomplish all God wants him to accomplish in the ministry.

There are several options available when it comes to education, and you and the Lord must decide which is best for you. You can spend three years in an accredited Bible institute and stop, but this is not recommended (unless age is a real factor). You can take those three years and add two more at a Bible college to earn a degree. Or, you can spend four years in college and add three more at seminary. Some men will feel called to earn graduate degrees, but be careful not to use school as an escape from the realities of the ministry. It is easy to die by degrees!

Whatever course of study you follow, just be sure you graduate knowing how to use the basic tools of the ministry. A working knowledge of the Bible is basic. Try to get hold of the basics of the Bible languages, even though you may plan to use interlinear translations and lexicons. Several good courses in preaching are essential. Learn how to prepare and present a message from the Word! Your basic courses in theology will help you recognize heresy when you see it, and will also keep you from confusion and contradiction in your preaching. History and philosophy may be dry, but they will give you perspective and depth.

Of course, you must be a student all of your life! Everything the pastor experiences or reads becomes a part of his spiritual treasury, and he can invest it in the work of the Lord. He will major on *The* Book, but he will also read books. He will read the "Book of Nature" and the "Book of Humanity" as well. He will constantly find that place where truth touches life, and there he will feed his people the eternal truth in Jesus Christ.

To sum it up: let God lead you to the school that will best prepare *you* for the work God has called *you* to do. While you are there, give yourself devotedly to your studies, because you will never see these years of preparation again. Do not look upon education as a parenthesis or a detour in your life, but as part of your obedience to the will of God. Scholarship is stewardship. You are ministering to the Lord in your studies as well as in your sermons, so be faithful. At some point you may be tempted to quit school and "get out into the work." Resist this temptation! Dr. W. B. Riley says it so well: "If your work in school makes a student of you, one of the essential preparations for preaching will have been accomplished. If you leave school with no love of study, the background of school will be of little value" (*The Preacher and His Preaching* [Wheaton, Ill.: Sword of the Lord, 1948], p. 21).

Does God call a man permanently to the ministry?

"No man, having put his hand to the plough, and looking back, is fit for the kingdom of God" (Lk 9:62). The emphasis throughout the Bible seems to be on a permanent call. *Please do not enter the ministry with reservations!* It is unwise to ask God for an escape clause in the contract. The couple that enters marriage saying, "Well, if it doesn't work, we can always get a divorce!" is asking for trouble; and so is the pastor who says to himself, "If I don't make it, I can always get a different job."

The ministry is not "a job" — it is a divine calling! "For the gifts and calling of God are without repentance" (Ro 11:29). The called man who tries to run away will, like Jonah, discover that there is no place to hide.

This does not mean that God will never change a man's sphere of ministry. Many a faithful pastor has been led from the local church ministry into teaching, missionary work, Bible conference ministry, or denominational responsibilities. Sometimes a crisis in the home requires a change of ministry. More than one man has had to change his sphere of service in order to care for an invalid wife or aged parents.

Every servant of God has, at one time or another, sensed his personal inadequacy for the work of the ministry. "No day passes," wrote the great Marcus Dods in his diary, "without strong temptation to give up, on the ground that I am not fitted for pastoral work. Writing sermons is often the hardest labor; visiting is terrible." Yet Marcus Dods became a great force for God, and pastors still read his books today.

When that hour comes and you feel like giving up — *Don't!* God has called you, God is with you, and God is going to use you to accomplish His purposes. Get alone with God and instead of resigning from the work, re-sign your holy vows! "Being confident of this very thing, that he which hath begun a good work in you will perform it until the day of Jesus Christ" (Phil 1:6).

Should an older man consider a call to the ministry?

There seems to be little evidence that the call of God always falls on youth. Amos and Moses were apparently settled in their vocations when God called them to preach. In fact, there are some advantages that the older man has that younger men may not possess: experience in life, seriousness of purpose, a maturity that education alone can never impart, a sense of values. Many educators claim that their older students really do far better than the young ones, if only because they have to try harder!

Of course, there are some disadvantages: the high cost of pulling up stakes and starting a new life; the ever-rolling stream of time, attachment to things and perhaps an affluent way of life, the difficulty of becoming a student again. But each of these so-called stumbling blocks can become a stepping-stone to the man who believes God. The important thing is not a man's age, but his willingness to obey God regardless of the cost.

In many respects, age is a state of mind. Cultivate the faith outlook on life, and you will always be young in heart and spirit. A desk motto we once read said: "Growing old is nothing but a bad habit which a busy man has no time to acquire."

What part does the wife, or fiancee, play in this matter of a call to the ministry?

She plays a very important part! The wife is to be a help and not a hindrance. Certainly a sovereign God, knowing He would call a man into His service, would also direct him to choose a wife that would be a "help meet [suitable] for him" (Gen 2:18). The problems of the ministry are great, and to add to them the burden of a divided household would but make them greater.

If a man is engaged to a Christian girl who does not feel the same calling to service, then let him break the engagement; or let her seek the Lord's will and surrender, if that is what is needed. "Can two walk together, except they be agreed?" (Amos 3:3).

The man already married faces a different — and more difficult — problem. If the wife is a good homemaker and a loving mate, there should be no problem; because the pastor's wife is first of all a "keeper at home." She need not be a stirring banquet speaker, a gifted musician, or a successful teacher to be a good pastor's wife. If she can keep the "home machinery" running smoothly so that her husband can fulfill his ministry, she will accomplish the most important task.

Unfortunately, some books written especially for the pastor's wife would frighten her out of her wits! Let her talk and pray with some experienced "mother in Israel" before she decides she is unfit for the ministry. God knows the heart, and many of the things people write about in books just never happen.

There should be agreement and harmony in the home. But this is true of *all* Christian homes, not just the pastor's home; so if a call to the ministry brings about violent reactions, something may be radically wrong with the basic structure of the home. Better these things are worked out lovingly and patiently, preferably under the guidance of a mature pastor.

More than one pastor has gotten along without help from his wife, but you cannot but feel sorry for them, and for their children. "It is not good that the man should be alone"

(Gen 2:18). "Two are better than one" (Ec 4:9). Poor John Wesley was married to a paranoid who refused to live with him or share his ministry. But then, what wife would want to spend her life (as Wesley did) on horseback? Of course, the married man must consider any children that are involved (1 Ti 5:8). God does not usually tear one thing down in order to build another thing up.

When marriage vows precede ordination vows, the laying on of hands does not automatically cancel them. A man may have to settle for "second best" if he discoverrs he has married out of the will of God. Let him then do his best to the glory of God and find encouragement in God's word to David: "Forasmuch as it was in thine heart . . . thou didst well in that it was in thine heart" (2 Ch 6:8).

I am a pastoral dropout. How can I get back into service again?

Begin, after much heart searching and prayer, by counseling with a pastor you know and trust. Some of the questions you must answer honestly are Why did I drop out? Has the problem been solved successfully? Am I now in the place of God's blessing so He can use me again? Have I taken the necessary steps to repair any damage I have done? Are there any character weaknesses that need to be dealt with before I can pastor again?

John Mark was a dropout, and God restored him and used him greatly. Even the great apostle Paul had to change his opinion about Mark! (Read Ac 15:36-41, Col 4:10, and 2 Ti 4:11.) Both Jonah and Peter failed in their calling, yet God forgave them and restored them. "And He made it again, another vessel" (Jer 18:1-4).

Above all else, rest on God's Word, not the opinions of men. David expressed a great truth when he said, after he had sinned, "Let me fall now into the hand of the Lord; for very great are his mercies: but let me not fall into the hand of man" (1 Ch 21:13). Sometimes other pastors can be very discouraging and condemning! God has promised to forgive (1 Jn 1:9) and to restore to fellowship and blessing. Rest on His promises!

Don't jump into the first opportunity for service that comes your way. Be sure you serve in the place of God's choosing. You cannot afford another crisis and failure. Perhaps working with an experienced pastor for a time would help you get back on your feet. "Watch and pray!" Satan is out to defeat and devour all of us! It is not necessary to assume that you will fail again; in fact, a defeatist attitude would assure such failure. But it is necessary to heed 1 Corinthians 10:12.

2

THE CALL TO A CHURCH

What steps should I take in finding a place to minister?

Ephesians 2:10 indicates that God prepares us for what He has prepared for us; so, if we are called of the Lord, He has a place for us to serve. Most beginning pastors start in a small place and then God leads them into larger fields of ministry. A few are called into larger spheres almost from the beginning, but this is not God's usual procedure (Mt 25:21).

We assume that you have been busy serving the Lord during your years of preparation, and that from this experience you have discovered and developed your gifts and abilities. "Know thyself" is an important admonition for the preacher of the Word, if he would not find himself in the wrong place doing the wrong job.

Be available! Never look upon any assignment or opportunity as a "small place." It has well been said, "Make every occasion a great occasion, for you can never tell when someone may be measuring you for a bigger place." The man who is too proud to preach to a small congregation will never preach to the large congregation successfully. Joshua got his start as Moses' servant, and David killed the lion and the bear in private before God permitted him to slay the giant in public. If you are a *called* man, and a *prepared* man, then be an *available* man and God will open and close doors for you.

It would be wonderful if every beginning pastor could

20

work for a year or two with an experienced man — not to imitate him, but to learn from him. It is much easier if you can be somewhat protected when you make your mistakes! Serving as an assistant pastor may not have the glamor of shepherding your own flock, but it does present several advantages. We already have suggested that an experienced pastor will help you over the rough spots and cover for you when you make your inevitable mistakes. This arrangement is also good for the family: they move gradually into pastoral work and have an easier time finding themselves. During a year or two of assisting ministry, the new pastor can develop study habits, learn how to visit, and learn how to conduct funerals and weddings. As a spectator at church business meetings, he can learn a great deal! If his pastor is wise, he will include him in the church councils on occasion; but the assistant must be careful to keep confidence at all times.

If no door of ministry opens immediately, don't give up. The great Bible scholar Marcus Dods waited for six years before a church would call him! During that time he preached, studied, mastered the Word, and waited for God's time. When the door finally opened, it led into a lifetime of fruitful service.

God often uses men to direct us into His will. Let some of your pastor friends know you are open to God's leading, and perhaps they can make suggestions. Often churches contact other pastors when they are seeking a shepherd; and while we do not lean on the arm of flesh, we do permit God to use other believers to give us guidance along the way.

Positively the worst thing you can do is promote yourself and try to push your way into some choice pulpit. "A man's gift maketh room for him," counseled Solomon (Pr 18:16), and good counsel it is. To use denominational politics to secure a call is to give evidence that you have no confidence in the promises of God or the power of prayer. Faith is *living without scheming;* and the sooner the new pastor learns this, the better. Nehemiah "prayed to God, and said to the king" (Neh 2:4-5) — and his priorities were correct! If you are walking with God, He will lead you to the right men and the right place of ministry.

These suggestions apply primarily to pastors in fellowships or denominations in which the local churches are free to call their own leaders. Men belonging to denominations that operate differently will perhaps find little help in these suggestions. Our own experience has been in the independent tradition, and we hesitate to give counsel outside the sphere of our own experience.

What do you do when you meet with a church pulpit committee?

Usually the members of the committee have already heard you preach, so you are not total strangers. Go to the meeting with a warm, loving spirit and ask for God's direction. Determine to be a blessing and all will go well.

The purpose of the meeting, of course, is for them to get acquainted with you and for you to find out about the church and its ministry. Here are some guidelines to follow:

Before the meeting. Read whatever literature is available about the church and its program. This especially includes the church constitution and bylaws, as well as a history of the church if one is available. The committee should share the budget with you as well. If none is available, write out the pertinent questions about finances that you want to ask. If you come with a set of important questions, you will keep the meeting on target and save a great deal of time and energy. Of course, the chairman of the meeting ought to have a definite agenda; but not every church knows this! It is wise to be prepared.

During the meeting. The committee will want to hear your personal testimony and any report of your ministry you can give. They may ask you for references, and so be prepared with a list of names and addresses. It would be helpful to have a typed resume that you can leave with the committee. Be sure to listen! And carefully answer every question with a sweet Christian spirit. This first contact with the key people of the church ought to be on a high level; for, if you become their pastor, you already have begun well! Be sure that every area is covered, and don't be ashamed to discuss finances. Take notes! This will save misunderstanding and embarrassment later on. Ask the committee to clarify any matters of church ministry that are not clear to you.

Do not make an impetuous decision to accept or reject the call at this preliminary meeting. Be sure to leave the meeting with a wholesome attitude, and thank the committee for their time and their help.

After the meeting. It is up to the committee to make a statement to you by letter, either asking you to consider the church, or informing you that they will be looking elsewhere. If they invite you to consider the church, it would be wise to return to the field, preach several times, and take more time to meet the people and consider the situation. "He that believeth shall not make haste" (Is 28:16). Be sure that all the details relating to the call are clearly spelled out in a formal letter: salary, housing, moving expenses (the church should pay these), responsibilities, vacation privileges, et cetera. It is better to have these defined in advance than debated on arrival!

Certainly you will spend much time in prayer, seeking the mind of the Lord. Feel free to contact the committee chairman if you need to discuss any matter. Even if they do not call you, this experience can be a means of spiritual growth, and it might open other doors. If no call comes, *do not become resentful.* Continue to pray for the church, that God will send them the man of His choice.

Perhaps a few don'ts would be in order.

Don't major on minors. Keep to the basics — the important things.

Don't argue with the committee about *anything!* If they are not scriptural in some matter, you can state your case lovingly; but don't turn the meeting into a debate.

Don't expect everything to be perfect. Churches are made up of people, and people are human. Only God never makes mistakes.

Don't criticize the church, the service, or the building. These people love their church, and you should love it, too — warts and all!

Don't resent being looked upon as a beginner. Some of the committee members have been around a long time and have interviewed many pastoral candidates. If at first they do not recognize your maturity and genius, be patient; if the gifts are there, God will make them known in His good time.

Don't make the mistake of thinking that all pulpit committees are alike, and that "if you've been to one meeting, you've been to them all." You will meet cautious committees, afraid to step out by faith; divided committees that do not know what kind of man the church needs; and fearful committees, ready to call the first man they see. Give yourself time to sense the atmosphere of the meeting, and you will come away feeling better.

The important thing is this: trust God to use the committee and to give you all the guidance you need. They will make mistakes; they will display prejudice and perhaps even ignorance; but God is still on the throne, and your trust is in Him.

How can I know that God has called me to minister in a specific church?

When you come to the place of God's choosing, several things will be true in your own heart. First, you will have a sense of belonging. More than one pastor has said, when coming to a new church situation, "I feel like I've been here all my life." Then, you will have that peace of God in your heart that Colossians 3:15 promises. As you read the Word and pray in your daily quiet time, the Spirit will impress on you, "This is the way, walk ye in it."

You will have a burden for the work. If you are moving from another pastorate, you will experience a lifting of the burden from that work and a growing burden for the new work. This may happen over a period of time, or it may come suddenly. Usually, there is a time of preparation when God weans the pastor away from one church and directs him into another work.

The possibilities — yes, even the problems — of the prospective pastorate will challenge and excite you. The existence of serious problems in a work is no reason to leave it (Titus 1:5 settles that), and neither is it a reason to avoid it. You do not have to agree totally with all the organization and structure of a church to be its pastor. Perhaps God has called you there to set something in order in due time. Of course, you and the church ought to agree doctrinally.

Most pastors like to talk over these decisions with pastor friends whom they love and trust. But do not talk to too many people. Share your decisions with your most trusted counselors and pray together for God's direction. Often, other Christians who know and love us will ratify the leading God gives us in our own hearts.

Never accept a church because there is no place to go, or because you have problems in your present ministry. Unsolved problems in the old ministry have a way of appearing in the new ministry! The man who keeps hopping from church to church because of problems never matures in his ministry because he keeps running from the very challenges that can make him grow. The pastor who moves because of problems in his church is like the girl who gets married in

order to leave home: both discover bigger problems in the
new place.

These big decisions of life are often built upon the little
decisions that we make day after day; so keep your devotional
life at a high level, and God will show you His will.

Should I accept a call if the vote has not been unanimous?

Some churches do not have the word *unanimous* in their
vocabulary. In fact, many churches (sad to say) have a few
"sanctified obstructionists" in their membership whose purpose in life is to keep the church from ever having a unanimous vote on anything.

Your decision should be influenced by the size of the negative vote. Wisdom would dictate that there should be a com-
fortable majority to work with; but opposition does present a
challenge to a man of God. In fact, some who vote for you
may turn against you before you have been on the field very
long; and some of your opponents may become your most
loyal workers. If the negative vote is small, you can accept
the call with safety in God's will. But if there is a sizeable
and vocal minority, it would be wise to wait.

Many churches take the vote, and if the majority calls the
man, they make the vote unanimous. This is a standard procedure, but it leaves the new pastor with a false sense of unity.
You have a right to know whether or not there was a con-
siderable negative vote.

If you accept the call, *do not try to find out how people
voted.* Some will say to you, "Well, I voted against you, so
be careful!" Treat all of the people graciously and seek to
win their love and confidence. Pastor the whole church, not
just your admirers. You will have the joy of seeing the
church united one day, including the people who voted
against you.

Some pastors feel they have failed unless every vote is a unanimous one. If you have this attitude, you will lose much joy in the ministry. A pastor and his people must seek the Lord's direction and vote as they feel led. The majority must rule, and the minority must disagree without being disagreeable. If the majority is right, it must not adopt a "We are God's people" attitude. If the minority turns out to be right, it must not say, "We told you so!" The pastor's personal attitude in these matters is the key to church harmony and progress. If he becomes dictatorial, he will divide the church. If he exercises love and patience, he will unite the church.

3

THE PASTOR IN A NEW CHURCH

How can I get started on the right foot in a new place of ministry?

1. Ask God to give you a deepening love for your people. Get to know them; build a prayer list and remember your people before the throne of grace.

2. Get acquainted enthusiastically with the work of the church. Avoid criticism; there are two sides to every story. Learn to appreciate the people, the buildings, the traditions, even though later you may make changes.

3. As you get acquainted with the work, make a list of personal priorities. You cannot do everything at once; and some things, when they are done, will make it easier to accomplish other tasks. Turn this list of priorities into a prayer list. Ask God to give you the wisdom to understand the situation and to know when to begin to act.

4. Be patient! It is amazing what can be accomplished with patience and prayer. Some men think they must have record accomplishments during the first month of their ministry, and they begin to *use* the people instead of leading them. Ask God for patience and understanding.

5. Try to avoid comparing your new church with the one you just left. It is difficult to plow a straight furrow when you are looking back. Each situation is different because God's people are different. Principles of ministry never change, but methods do change from place to place. If you constantly

28

compare one church with another, you will gradually become critical; and a critical pastor has a hard time loving his people.

6. Visit your people, especially the elderly people, the shut-ins, and the church leaders. The elderly will appreciate your visits, and their loved ones will thank you for caring. These people may be among the first to die, and it is good to know them before you conduct the funeral. The shut-in members and friends will be your greatest prayer partners. And it is good to be in the homes of church leaders, because knowledge of the homes will help you in understanding the people themselves. You may be more patient with a deacon when you discover the burdens he bears at home.

7. Preach heartening messages from the great passages in the Word. Many men prefer to preach through a book, or in an announced series. This approach disarms the critical members who want to accuse you of preaching against certain sins in the church. If controversial topics like divorce or church divisions do come up, they cannot accuse you of selecting your topics.

8. Take advantage of your newness to visit as many people as possible. "I'm the new pastor at First Church!" is a key to open doors for several months, but eventually you will have to hang up the key and take a new approach. Visit members who have dropped out; visit the unsaved and try to win them; visit the parents of Sunday school children. Your ministry will be more personal if you take time to visit in the homes.

9. Don't believe everything you hear. In fact, when people start to criticize, gently ask them not to. In time, word will get around that the new pastor does not encourage gossip. This does not mean you should turn a deaf ear to a trusted officer who wants to warn you about a persistent problem person. But it does mean you do not categorize people on the basis of the prejudices of a few members. That family that did not respond to the last pastor's ministry may really get "turned on" when they hear you preach. You will

hear both good and bad about many people. Don't commit yourself; let God direct you.

10. You do not *demand* respect; you *command* it. Your people want to love you and follow you, but they need time to get to know you. Once you have won their love and respect, they will be willing to follow your leadership. Quietly go to work winning the lost, organizing the work, building the saints, and moving the church into wider ministries; and in time, God's blessing will win for you the respect and cooperation you desire.

11. Plan to stay! Your desire to stay with the people, in spite of their faults (and yours), will endear you to them that much more. Let it be known that you want to do a solid work in the church and not merely visit them for a year or so "until something better opens up."

12. Pray for your leaders by name regularly. Ask God to make them spiritual. Let them know privately that you do pray for them, and ask them to share their special needs with you.

13. When that first crisis comes, face and handle it as though you had been there ten years. Exercise love and kindness, and obey the Word of God. The way you do things the first time will determine the way you do them the second and third time. Once your people realize that you mean business, they will respond with appreciation and cooperation. The others will either pout or leave.

14. As your plans materialize, talk them over privately with your leaders. They have a right to know where you are going. Don't pressure them into moving quickly. "Be calm in thy soul." Pressured people usually respond negatively. Where there is calmness and a sense of direction, people will respond positively.

It takes time to build a spiritual church, so don't become frustrated if things don't change overnight. Good beginnings usually mean good endings, so watch your beginnings.

15. Stay close to home that first year on the field. Once you have established yourself in your ministry, you will have plenty of opportunities to minister in other places from time to time. But don't become a guest speaker in your own pulpit!

16. Get to know the other pastors in your area. Some of them will become your closest friends and will remain close even after you leave the field. Be friendly to all, even those with whom you may disagree. You may not want them in your pulpit, but don't exclude them from your friendship and prayers.

I feel God has called me to a specific church, but there are things about the work that desperately need changing. How do I go about changing things?

The man who feels he must agree completely with a church program before he will accept a call is doomed to disappointment and defeat in the ministry. Of course, there must be agreement in basic doctrine and polity; but it is not necessary for the pastor to feel that *everything* must be his way. Many good pastors will tell you after years of ministry in one church that there are still undesirable practices and situations that have not been changed; yet they have been able to minister with blessing.

Begin by creating an atmosphere of love and confidence. This takes time, prayer, and a great deal of sacrifice. If you are a servant of the people for Jesus' sake, you soon will become their leader. As we mentioned before, we do not *demand* respect; we *command* it.

Distinguish between your own pet desires and real basic needs. If you make changes just to suit yourself, you are being selfish and shortsighted. Changes should be made in order to make the ministry more spiritual, or to improve the ministry of the church. Change for the sake of change is novelty, and you cannot build a strong work on novelty. Nor can you afford to be experimenting constantly. As we suggested before, have a list of priorities and let them be your guide.

Make as few changes as possible, and be sure they are basic and not merely surface changes. Also, make sure they are biblical!

It is often good policy to ask the church to try things out for a short period of time. If the trial works, fine; if not, nothing is lost. People are usually willing to try something out provided they are not committed for life!

Timing is important, so don't be impatient. Remember that you are making changes for the good of the ministry, not for the glory of the minister.

Win the confidence of the people, introduce your plans with "we ought" rather than "you ought," and be careful of the big stick. If the sheep are *fed,* they may be *led;* but no sheep likes to be driven.

How does the pastor really become the leader in the church?

He becomes the leader by taking the position of leader with humility and using his office for the good of others and the glory of God. The church does not make him their leader; God does. "Ourselves your servants for Jesus' sake." The Lord Jesus Christ was a great Pastor: "He goeth before them, and the sheep follow him: for they know his voice" (Jn 10:4).

Read 1 Peter 5 and John 13-17, and let these principles of spiritual leadership burn themselves into your soul. We lead by love and humility, not by hatred and force. We lead by setting the example. The Pharisees were harder on the people than they were on themselves, but not so the New Testament pastor. Before he preaches, he practices.

We lead through the Word and prayer. When the sheep are fed, they are usually happy to follow! We lead through sacrificial service (read Philippians 2) — by paying a price.

John Henry Jowett said that ministry that costs nothing accomplishes nothing.

We lead "in season and out of season." In our personal friendly conversations with our people, as well as in business meetings, we show that we can be trusted. The casual street-corner conversation with an officer can be more effective than next Sunday's sermon, if the Lord is in it!

We lead by accepting responsibility and being faithful. Matters like being early to appointments, always having an agenda, giving credit where it is due, and admitting mistakes go a long way toward winning the respect of the people.

We pastors need to remember that our people have had different experiences with former pastors; and some of those experiences have left wounds. It is understandable that some church members will be cautious when it comes to accepting and following a new pastor. Here is where patience and love come in.

How can we tell when we are finally moving into that place of spiritual leadership that we desire? For one thing, the machinery of the church will move a bit faster and smoother. There will still be opposition — and loyal opposition has its place in a congregational government — but opposition will not be a threat. The people will be far more open, especially in their disagreements. It is a good sign when church members can feel free to disagree with their pastor in the right spirit. The pastor will feel at home in the administrative work of the church. He will understand the hearts and minds of his leaders and be better able to work with them. In turn, they will have a clearer grasp of their pastor's plans and purposes.

Leadership must never be exploited for personal gain. It is always used for the good of the church and the glory of God. "The chief is servant of all," says an African proverb. Jesus said, "He that is greatest among you shall be your servant" (Mt 23:11). As you gain in leadership *abilities,* you will also

gain in leadership *opportunities*. God does not want you or
the church to stand still! So, with increased leadership will
come increased opportunities for ministry; and these new opportunities will bring new demands, new challenges, and new
problems. But this is far better than constantly facing the
same old problems!

Stop at the nearest library and check the books available on
executive leadership and related themes. The children of this
world are wiser in these things than are the children of light.
Always balance men's ideas with God's wisdom. The book of
Nehemiah shows a true leader at work; and 2 Corinthians
gives you insight into the heart of Paul as he faces and solves
church problems. Read James 3:13—4:17, too.

How important is a church constitution? How can I go about making changes in an "antique" constitution?

All things should be done decently and in order. This is
the main purpose of a constitution. Many churches are incorporated, and thus a constitution and set of bylaws is de-
manded by law. But even if a church is not legally incorporated, it needs organizational guidelines or else its activities
will create chaos.

The mistake churches make about the constitution is in
thinking that a good constitution makes a good church. They
try to put everything in the constitution they can think of —
every possible emergency and need — and thus create a mon-
ster. The constitution is the track on which the train runs;
it is not the steam in the boiler. One well-known pastor accepted his church on the condition that they "put the constitution away for a whole year and use only the Bible in gov-
erning the church." It worked! In fact, it is likely that the
constitution has not been taken out of hiding since!

The constitution cannot make the church spiritual, any

more than the Ten Commandments could make Israel spiritual. This is a work God alone can do in the heart through
the Spirit's use of the Word. The danger of legalism is always
present, particularly in groups that want to have high standards for their church. But adding new articles to the constitution — or deleting articles — will never change the
church. This can only improve (or hinder) the organizational working of the church.

Be sure to read the constitution carefully before accepting
a church. If you have differences, discuss them freely with
the official committee. Sometimes it is a matter of interpreta-
tion rather than principle. If God leads you to accept the
church, live with the constitution and respect it; but begin to
pray and plan toward changes. Be sure, however, that you
are operating from a position of leadership before you suggest
any changes; and give the leaders opportunity to think things
through. If your preaching and pastoring have created an
atmosphere of love and trust, the church will be willing to
consider your ideas. Be sure you can back up your suggestions with the principles of the Word, but expect to find a
few members who feel that the constitution is as inspired as
the Bible!

It is wise to make changes in the constitution all at once and
not piecemeal. If a church is repeatedly voting on new articles, members become frustrated and weary of the whole
matter. Give yourself time to read and digest the whole constitution, decide what changes *really* must be made, and take
care of all the surgery at once. Be a Christian statesman in
the whole matter, and don't split your church over issues that
are not important. If you discover something disagreeable
after coming to the church — something you could have known
about before coming — please don't take it out on the church.
Commit it to God; pray about it; and at the right time, discuss
it with your leaders.

No matter what the church organization may be, the pastor should be the spiritual leader of the congregation. 1 Peter 5:1-3, Hebrews 13:7, 1 Thessalonians 5:12, and 1 Timothy 3:5 indicate this. There are many areas within the church organization where gifted men and women will exercise better leadership than the pastor, because God has so gifted them; but the flock should be under his direction. This does not mean that he must preside at every meeting. Our experience in the ministry has been with independent local churches where the pastor is the moderator of the meeting; but we recognize the fact that a gifted layman could be moderator or president without usurping the God-given responsibilities of the pastor. If your conviction is that the pastor should preside, and the church considering you has a different arrangement, then you owe it to the church and to yourself to examine the matter carefully. You may create constant friction unless there is some mutual understanding.

I dislike committee meetings! Since I *have* to attend, how can I develop a better attitude toward this part of my work?

Don't make the mistake of dividing your work between spiritual and organizational or administrative; there is no such division. No matter what kind of meeting you are attending — a prayer meeting or a business meeting — you are pastoring the church. Once you begin to wear more than one hat (pastor and administrator), you will start to have headaches in both heads!

The church is an organism; but the church is also an organization. And if an organism is not organized, it will die! Paul's example in Acts and his teachings in the epistles would indicate that he believed in establishing local churches in an organized way. It is when organization becomes an end in itself, and not a means to an end, that the church becomes institutional and starts to die. Organization is to the church what the scaffolding is to a building under construction: it helps get the job done.

So, your first step is to get the right perspective or organizational meetings. Look upon them as opportunities to pastor your leaders and help them grow spiritually. Never attend a committee meeting looking like a man expecting an execution! Approach the meeting in the fullness of the Spirit with a desire to apply the Word of God to living situations. Often you will accomplish more good in the life of the church in a committee meeting than you will in a preaching service! The organizational functions of the church are opportunities for you to practice what you preach — and perhaps that is what makes them so dreadful!

Maintain a close relationship with your key leaders. Your personal ministry to them in private as a pastor-friend will help establish wholesome relationships in public meetings. This does not mean that the pastor tries to "win friends and influence people" or "politicks" outside the business meetings, because such a practice would be insincere and unspiritual. It does mean that he develops a warm, loving relationship with his leaders so that they can discuss matters and even disagree without becoming enemies.

There is an art to running a meeting; and, alas, some church officers have never had the opportunity to learn it. So teach them! Remind them that a good meeting always starts on time, has a prepared agenda, stays on target, and seeks to end on time. "Work expands to fill the amount of time available for it." Give the average committee three hours for a meeting, and they will consume all three hours. Give them thirty minutes, and they will probably be able to reach the same conclusions! It takes time, but church leaders can be taught how to conduct a good meeting and get things done. But don't do your correcting in public unless absolutely necessary. Talk to any problem people privately; they will appreciate your kindness.

G. Campbell Morgan used to have a policy, "The minimum of organization for a maximum of work." It pays to examine your organizational structure regularly to see if some of the scaffolding can be taken down. Be slow to create new committees; use existing organizations as much as possible.

Prayer lubricates the machinery of the church. It has been our experience that business meetings (and their length) decrease as prayer increases. Be sure to meet at least once a month with your officers for a time of serious prayer. Pray about *specific* needs in the church and face problems honestly. You will be surprised at what the Spirit will do!

It takes time for a new pastor to "get acquainted" with the machinery of the church. It also takes time for any pastor to develop his leadership abilities. Do not permit mistakes or hurts from the past to hinder you from a happy ministry today. Watch out for that conditioned reflex many pastors experience when their ideas are rejected. Learn to lose graciously. Chances are that some member of the board will remember your idea, think about it, present it at the next meeting as his own — and it will be accepted! There is no limit to what a pastor can accomplish in a church if he does not care who gets the credit! If God has directed you to the church and burdened you to accomplish certain things, then He will see you through if you will just be loving and patient. You may lose a few battles, but eventually you will win the war.

Because of some past scandals and problems, the church I pastor has a bad name in our community. How do I go about restoring the good name of the church?

Be a good man in the community, and the people will take notice. In fact, they will probably give thanks that a new man has come, for a church with a bad name cannot help but give the community some embarrassment. The fine people of the community will be behind you, so take heart.

Find out how much of the past still lingers in the church. Work with individuals; pray out the poison. Ask God to help you create a sweet, loving spirit in the church. "Love covers a multitude of sins." Word soon will get out that something new and wonderful is happening, and the contrast will be good promotion for you!

In the midweek service and in official meetings, teach your people to uphold the church. "Forgetting those things which are behind" ought to be the motto of the congregation. As you teach the Word, it will cleanse and renew the people; so major on the positive. We have said it before: be patient!

Finally, use advertising judiciously. Notices in the newspapers will let people know that the church is still ministering and that a new era has begun. Be sure that nothing negative ever appears in your printed materials, such as the church bulletin. Other people read these things — and talk.

Bringing spiritual health to a sick church body is a great challenge. But what a joy it is when the health returns and the body starts to grow! It takes love, patience, prayer, and a solid ministry of the Word. Settle it in your mind that you will stay with it until the job is done. If the church changes pastors again, it might mean total defeat. "If God be for us, who can be against us?"

I grew up in the city, but I will be pastoring in a rural area. What should I know so I will do a good job?

First, don't minimize the importance of the rural ministry. Our villages and small towns make up one of the greatest mission fields in the world today. If it is right for a missionary to seek out scattered small villages in some primitive area, why is it wrong for a man to minister in a village in America or Canada?

Generally speaking, the life style is different from that in the big city, although city ways are entering into country life. The people of the soil are generally more relaxed, more patient, and more serious. They take time to get to know each other. They look beneath the surface. For the most part, they accept the pastor who is real, sincere, and loving, regardless of where he grew up.

Rural churches resist pressure and high-powered promotion. You will want to study their habits and try to enter into their thinking, but you would do this in any church situation. Don't try to make the rural program conform to that of the big city. Farm people live close to the seasons, and you will want to do the same. What the church does must fit into the daily work schedule of the members and not just the ideas of the pastor.

People live miles from each other in many farm areas; and when they come to church, they want to have time to visit. Your own visitation program must take these distances into consideration. While in the city you can make brief visits in apartments; in the country your people will want you to stay awhile. And they probably will want your wife to visit with you as much as possible.

Ministering in the small community has its advantages and disadvantages. Sometimes one or two families (usually intermarried) will get control of a church and the pastor must deal with power blocs. Everybody knows everybody else's business, and the past is not easily forgotten. Traditions are held tenaciously, but this also happens in city churches. The beginning pastor, however, will usually discover a nucleus of godly people who will love him, encourage him, and make him glad he tarried with them.

Get acquainted with funeral and marriage customs early in your ministry. Learn the "lore of the land" by talking with

and listening to the old timers in the area. Be genuinely interested, and your own life will be enriched.

Give the people the very best that you have; feed them the
finest of the wheat. Never judge your ministry by the number
of people who show up, although you do want the work to
grow. The potential in many rural areas is not great, but
this should not encourage you to do less than your best. Especially get to know the children and young people. Many
of them will perhaps move into the cities when they get older,
so minister to them while you have opportunity. Those who
marry and stay home should be worked into the local church
ministry. Those who move away should be encouraged to get
into good churches in the cities.

Never give the impression you are ministering there until
something bigger comes along. Be devoted to your people;
and if God does open a larger door, you will be ready to enter
it. In the years to come you will be grateful for the opportunity He gave you to establish your spiritual roots in a rural
area.

4

CHURCH ORGANIZATION

Is there any divine pattern of church organization?

Any honest student of church history must confess that God has used and blessed men in just about every form of church government: congregational, presbyterian, and episcopal! Reorganizing your church is not a guarantee that God will send revival.

Acts 6:1-7 indicates that the early church was basically congregational, but that it respected the oversight of the spiritual leaders. 1 Timothy 3 indicates that the two fundamental officers in the church were bishops (overseers) and deacons. A comparison of Acts 20:17 and 28 suggests that the terms *bishop* and *elder* are synonymous, and are equivalent to pastor. Some churches have the pastor as the leader of the church, the elders as spiritual leaders with him, and the deacons as officers who manage the financial and physical operation of the ministry. If the church is incorporated, it must have trustees.

Regardless of what officers you elect, and what you call them, the church must have leadership. Church organization must not become a substitute for the work of the Spirit in the church. One pastor has said, "If God were to take the Holy Spirit out of the world, most of what we are doing would go right on and nobody would know the difference!" A sobering thought. Organization should be a blessing, not a burden; a means of getting work done, not hindering it. The size of the congregation pretty well determines the amount of organization the church needs.

Accept the organization as you find it. If the Lord convinces you there are areas that are not scriptural, discuss it with your key leaders and give them time to pray and reflect. But don't get the idea that a certain kind of organization automatically wins the blessing of God! God blesses men, not machinery.

How do I go about finding and training leadership in the church?

Preach the Word faithfully. The Word feeds and equips the saints to do the work of the ministry (2 Ti 3:16-17, Eph 4:11-12). It also sifts the people and causes dead wood to drop out. Back up your messages with prayer, and pray for your people *by name.* Jesus commanded us to pray for laborers (Lk 10:2).

It is usually unwise to advertise for workers. Often the cranks show up and then you have to find something for them to do. Quietly watch the congregation and God will give you direction. If you think a member has potential, try him out in a small place (Mt 25:21 again!) and let him prove himself. Take men visiting with you and see how they handle themselves in homes. (This is also the best way to train soulwinners.)

When you do challenge a man to fill an office, *don't make it sound easy!* Tell him it will be demanding and require spiritual discipline. Communists never ask a man to do an easy job. They make it hard — and they get the recruits! Capable men respond to a challenge, no matter how difficult it may be. Lesser men enjoy *filling* an office but do not plan to *use* it.

Many churches have effectively used talent inventory sheets

that list dozens of opportunities for service. (Remember, there are *many* spiritual gifts.) Each new member ought to be given a copy of the inventory, and it would not hurt to survey the entire membership annually. There are leadership training courses and teacher training courses available from several evangelical publishers; so check with your denomination or your local Christian bookseller.

The Timothy system still works (2 Ti 2:2). Carefully select a young man in the church, and share yourself with him. Disciple him! When he is trained, let him help you train others. This plan takes time, but it finally multiplies the leaders in the church. However, be prepared to see several of these called into Christian service, and rejoice that your ministry will be multiplied that much more.

How do you go about removing "dead" officers and teachers?

This is one area that demands a great deal of prayer and patience. Most churches lack the dedicated leadership needed, and removing willing workers (even if they are incompetent) seems like suicide. But keep in mind that *we reproduce after our kind.* One poor teacher could manufacture in his class a dozen difficult church members or equally unqualified teachers. What do we do?

First, always aim for excellence in your ministry, and challenge your workers to aim for excellence. Create an atmosphere of excellence, and before long some of the incompetents will feel uncomfortable.

Second, make it easy for people to resign or change ministries. Many churches have found it helpful to survey their entire teaching staff once a year to see if any of the members want to take a year's "furlough" or move to a different department. It is amazing what happens to a teacher when she is liberated from twenty-one years of confinement in the nursery department! Better to unite a couple of classes and give them a teacher who enjoys the work and does it well, than to make one class suffer with a malcontent.

Begin a program of in-service training, with assistant teachers in each department. The assistants should be given opportunity to teach regularly, and the teacher should help train them. Often a poor teacher will sense he is out of place and will want to give the class to the assistant. Just be sure that such transitions are without competition or embarrassment.

When you feel your own leadership is secure, suggest definite standards for teachers and officers. You will want to beware of setting up a pharisaical code, of course; but there is nothing wrong with a set of biblical standards for those who lead the church's ministry. A leadership training class or a teachers' training class is also valuable, especially if your code requires all future leaders to graduate from the course.

There is nothing like "fresh blood" to resurrect a dead committee or department, so try to work in your new converts and new members just as soon as they are ready. The usual problem is the unwillingness of some of the older members to relinquish their places. In some cases, a funeral seems to be the only answer! Take it to the Lord in prayer and let Him handle each case in His way and in His time.

Be sure you know your leaders personally before you start using surgery. The better you understand their lives and homes, the better you will know why they seem to be misfits, and where they can fit the best. Above all, don't try to remove a leader simply because he does not agree with you. Find out why he disagrees; he may have some legitimate disagreements! Of course, a persistent troublemaker must be dealt with (Titus 3:10-11).

Is there a biblical plan for church finances, and to what degree should the pastor be involved?

The biblical plan seems to be the bringing of tithes and offerings by the believers to the local assemblies (1 Co 16:1-3). 2 Corinthians 8-9 is a great passage to study on the matter of church finances. You will note that the giving was church-centered (8:1), from the heart (8:2-9), proportionate (8: 10-15), and handled honestly (8:16-24). The right kind of giving brings blessing to others (9:1-5), blessing to the giver (9:6-11), and glory to God (9:12-15). The emphasis in these chapters is on the *grace* of giving (8:1, 6-7, 9, 19, and 9:8).

If the sheep are properly fed, they may be "milked" and "shorn." Some pastors forget that the Bible shepherd kept his sheep for their wool and milk and for reproducing — not especially for their meat. For a pastor constantly to be "butchering the sheep" is tragic for the church. When God's people receive a balanced diet of spiritual food and service, they are only too glad to give.

It is our conviction that people should be taught to give *to* their local church and *through* their local church. It is unfortunate that there is so much competition for the evangelical dollar these days. If every believer were faithfully giving to his own local church, there would be "bread enough and to spare" for the local ministry and for sharing with other ministries. No pastor can force his people into any pattern of giving, nor should he want to. But it is unfortunate when church members send God's money all over the world and yet fail to support their own local church. Galatians 6:6 teaches that the believer should share material things with those who minister to him in spiritual things, and certainly this would include his home church.

Luke 16:1-12 indicates that there is a definite relationship between how a servant of God handles spiritual things and material things. More than one minister has lost his testimony and ruined his ministry because of the mishandling of funds. This explains why Paul was so careful to have messengers from the local churches when he carried the gift to the Jerusalem saints (2 Co 8:16-24). Things like budgets, finance committees, and audits may seem like red tape, but they are wonderful safeguards against the accusation that the pastor is not honest with church funds. The pastor ought to work closely with his officers in these matters. If the pastor is not concerned about the financial aspects of the church, it is doubtful whether the members will get under the burden.

Whatever you do, don't constantly harp about money! The expository preacher who leads his people through the green pastures of the Word will have many opportunities to teach Christian stewardship. Also, *don't bring personal finances into the pulpit.* We heard of one pastor who complained in a sermon that he had to "dip into his savings account" to buy a new suit. Many of his listeners did not even have a savings account.

Many churches hold a membership orientation class. This is a good place to share the financial needs of the church and teach new converts and new members the biblical principles of giving. Many churches mail out quarterly or annual statements of giving. A good tract about stewardship could be included. And don't overlook the possibilities of the members naming the church in their wills. Talk to a reputable stewardship man about setting up a will clinic in your church, or making estate information available to your members. It is not as difficult as it may seem.

J. Hudson Taylor was right: when God's work is done in God's way, for God's glory, it will never lack God's supply. God is not obligated to pay for our selfish schemes. He is obligated to support His ministry.

Is it right for a church to have a savings account when there are so many needs to be met, especially on the mission field?

It is not unscriptural to save money or to collect interest. In fact, Christ's parables of the talents of the pounds are built on that theme. Nor is it wrong for a church to plan for the future, provided it does not turn into a building and loan association and become so obsessed with money that it loses its spiritual values (Rev 3:17). In fact, the church that builds its savings and collects some interest will actually save money by not having to borrow.

As for missionary needs, these should be met as the Lord leads and enables; but nowhere does the Bible tell us to tear down the work at home in order to build it up somewhere else. Many mission boards have savings accounts as they plan for future expansion. The careful use of money is a spiritual ministry (Lk 16:1-12). "Not slothful in business" can be applied to matters financial as well as spiritual.

The key issues are motive and purpose. If your motive is right and the purpose is in God's will, then a savings account can be a blessing. Most churches had better keep a fund available, since the blowing up of a boiler or the sudden collapse of the electrical system could put the church out of business. Better to have an emergency fund on hand than to plead for help when the crisis arises.

Some churches include in their annual budget a set amount to be used for missionary emergencies only. The fund is controlled by the pastor and board, so it is not necessary to call a congregational meeting for approval. If a missionary needs emergency surgery, or must return home suddenly, the fund can help without hurting the total budget.

There seems to be a legalistic atmosphere in our church, with an emphasis on rules and regulations. I have nothing against biblical standards, but I am deathly afraid of Pharisaism getting in and killing the life of the church. What should I do?

Gilbert K. Chesterton used to say, "Never take down a fence until you know why it was put up." Often a church becomes legalistic in order to defend its ministry. Instead of trusting the Word, prayer, and the Spirit, church boards pass rules and turn pastors into policemen. In time, the rules become "as inspired as the Word," even though the situations that called them forth disappeared long ago. There is certainly nothing wrong with a church setting up biblical standards, just so long as they realize that the standards will not change anybody and that not everyone who obeys the standards is necessarily spiritual!

The tragedy of the legalistic spirit is that it generates criticism, and a critical church is a divided church. It also produces spiritual pride, and that we-are-better-than-any-other-church attitude.

We reproduce after our kind. A critical pastor gradually produces a church full of critical people — and they will criticize the pastor the most! A loving pastor will eventually create an atmosphere of love and acceptance. It is not necessary to fight the rules; just quietly go about your business and love the people, and the rules will gently sink into oblivion. This does not mean you lower the standards of the church. It means you *raise* the standards by giving the members a higher spiritual motive! Paul had some of this in mind when he wrote Romans 7:14 — 8:13.

There are three levels of obedience: fear, reward, and love. The lowest is fear — obeying because we have to. The next is reward — obeying because we get something out of it. The highest is love — obeying because we love Christ and our fellow Christians. Men do not become spiritual by constraint from the outside; it must come from compassion on the inside. In 2 Corinthians 3, Paul contrasts the legalistic ministry of the Old Testament and the Spirit's ministry in the new covenant. Every pastor ought to read and master Dr. A. T. Robertson's masterful exposition of this passage in *The Glory of the Ministry* (Grand Rapids, Mich.: Baker, 1967).

Nothing breaks the shackles of tradition like evangelism. Start to win souls, and the new babes in Christ will help create an exciting new atmosphere in the church. To be sure, the scribes and Pharisees will sit on the sidelines and criticize, defending their rules; but love them anyway, pray for them, and keep doing the job.

5

PREACHING

Is preaching really important to the ministry of the church?

Preaching is, of course, only one way God has given for the proclamation of His Word; but we sincerely believe it is the most important. We certainly proclaim His Word at the Lord's Table and in baptism, as well as in the spiritual ministries of the individual believer ("Let your light so shine . . ."); but there is really nothing that can take the place of the preaching of the Word of God in what we know as the sermon. When God would present His Son to the world, He sent a preacher named John the Baptist. Much of our Bible is made up of messages delivered by men of God. Whether we like it or not, the spiritual level of the church rises or falls with the preaching of the Word. Church members will tolerate almost anything in a pastor, but if he does not feed them and teach them, they will turn him off — and possibly turn him out! The pastor who does not believe in the importance of preaching, and who does not work at being a better preacher, is going to have a rough time. Perhaps he should serve as some preacher's assistant and develop the gifts God has given him.

How many politicians or educators could get crowds to come and hear them week after week, year after year? Yet millions of people each week go to church to hear a man preach the Word of God. G. Campbell Morgan called preaching "the supreme work of the Christian ministry." It is also the hardest work in the ministry, if it is done faithfully.

Why has preaching declined in recent years? For one thing, the churches have been too easily influenced by the latest secular fads — counseling, group dynamics, dialogue, drama, and so forth. While all these may have their place in the ministry of a church, none of them can adequately substitute for the preaching of God's Word. Men may be moved in one way or another by movies and drama, music and debate, but they will never be changed and lifted higher, apart from the proclamation of the Word of God.

Perhaps the main reason people have criticized preaching is the fact that so much preaching is poorly done and does not meet the needs of the people. The pastor who runs around town all week, making himself think he is busy, and who turns out a sermon on Saturday evening, is digging his own grave. Sad to say, he may take his church in with him! *Real preaching is hard work.* Perhaps this may explain why some pastors look for substitute ministries.

If preaching is important to you as a pastor, everybody will know it. They will know that you spend time daily studying the Word. They will see you visiting and counseling so that you are better acquainted with the needs of your people. They will sense that you are a man living by priorities. Most of all, when they hear you preach, their hearts will be helped and they will give thanks to you and to God that they have a pastor who loves them enough to work hard at preaching.

The next time you are tempted to question the centrality of preaching in your ministry, remember what the preaching of the Word accomplished in Martin Luther's Europe and John Wesley's England. Think of George Whitefield and Jonathan Edwards, Billy Sunday and Dwight L. Moody. And think of your hungry sheep who come week by week to be fed. Paul puts it so pointedly: "Woe is unto me, if I preach not the gospel!" (1 Co 9:16).

How can I improve my preaching?

Begin by never being satisfied with it or believing all the marvelous things people say about it. While we appreciate the encouragement that comes when a message helps a needy heart, we must never rest on our laurels and become complacent. After he had been in the ministry over a quarter of a century, Spurgeon told his congregation, "I am still learning how to preach." The satisfied preacher will never grow. He will become the center of a mutual admiration society, not a source of spiritual power.

We improve the preaching by improving the preacher. Phillips Brooks was right: preaching is the communication of divine truth through human personality (*Lectures on Preaching* [New York: Dutton, 1877], p. 5). "There was a man sent from God, whose name was John" (Jn 1:6). As we grow in grace and knowledge and cultivate a satisfying devotional life, we cannot help but improve our studies, our sermon preparation, and our delivery.

Don't be afraid of kind criticism. In the early days of his ministry, Spurgeon received a letter every Monday from an anonymous hearer, in which the man lovingly pointed out the preacher's errors on the previous day. Instead of resenting this constructive criticism, Spurgeon welcomed it and profited from it. Here is where a tape recorder comes in handy — if you can bear to listen to yourself! A faithful wife is also a helpful critic.

Hear other men as opportunities come your way — not only the well-known preachers, but local men who as yet have no fame. You can learn from every man, either what to do or what not to do. Many excellent preachers have sermons available on tapes and cassettes. Warning: don't become the blind disciple of some great man. Thou shalt not worship the tape recorder.

Read good books on preaching, and read sermons. George

Morrison used to read a sermon a day, selecting them from many different preachers. Read them for your own spiritual benefit first. Then read them for an understanding of the preacher's technique — his approach. Don't imitate him, but learn from him. John Henry Jowett confessed that he often asked in his studies, "How would Spurgeon deal with this text? How would Alexander Whyte lay hold of it?" He called this "looking at the theme through many windows" (*The Preacher: His Life and Work* [Garden City, N.Y.: Doran, 1912], pp. 127-28). By all means index all the sermons in your library so you can locate them quickly, read, and compare them.

Dare to move into new territory. Too many of us enjoy the preaching on our favorite themes, and we resist breaking new ground. Paul admonished Timothy to give himself wholly to the ministry and to meditate on the Word "that thy profiting may appear to all." That word *profiting* means pioneer advance. Paul wanted Timothy to pioneer into new spiritual territory! Beware of promoting homiletical hobbies.

There is a wealth of enriching spiritual food in the proper use of the original languages of the Bible. We say the *proper* use, because there is a wrong way to use Hebrew and Greek. Your people want the meal, not the recipe; and bombarding them with cognates and tenses and other grammatical artillery can take away their appetite for deeper spiritual things. There are many tools available today, even for the man who has not been able to master these languages. Devote yourself to their use and you cannot help but grow yourself, and help your people grow.

If you are sincere in wanting to improve your preaching, God will give you opportunities to do so. He will permit situations to come to your life that will drive you to the Word and prayer. One of the best places to read God's Word is in the furnace of affliction. When God wants to proclaim a message, He prepares a man. Be that man!

Can you give me some suggestions for effective sermon preparation?

Be yourself. Your *best* self, of course; but be yourself. Many of us prefer expository preaching, and we heartily recommend it to you. But many effective preachers were not expositors of the Word: Phillips Brooks and George W. Truett are two classic examples. Please don't imitate some great man and miss what God has planned for you. Learn from everyone, but be yourself.

Plan your preaching. Don't spend most of the week frantically hunting for something to say. Preach through a book, or give a series of messages on a connected theme: the prayers of the Bible, the parables, the miracles, or character studies. It is amazing how the Spirit uses messages in a series to meet needs that we did not know even existed. Don't become a slave to a plan, however. If some crucial event occurs — or if God burdens you to give a different message — by all means follow the Spirit's leading. In fact, interrupting a series will give the message that much more meaning. If you know where you are going week by week, you can be thinking ahead.

Start working early. If you are preaching through a book you can do your spadework on a larger section than you intend to preach from, and in that way get ahead for the subsequent weeks. Get started early in the week and early in the day. Give yourself some deadlines: aim to have both Sunday sermons in final form by Friday noon. Nothing is more frustrating than trying to get a week's work done on Saturday afternoon!

Be systematic. Many preachers use a desk portfolio to keep their notes in as they study. You can find these in your local stationer's. Have one page and pocket set aside for the Sunday morning message; another for the evening message; a third for your prayer meeting message, and so on. Take your notes on little pieces of paper, perhaps three inches by three inches, instead of regular sheets. Put only one idea or fact on each little note-size sheet. When the time comes to organize your notes all you have to do is sort out the papers!

Start with the Word. Before you turn to your books, concentrate on *the* Book. Get the message from the passage or text. Jot down the ideas the Spirit gives you. Use the original languages if possible; use several translations. Then turn to the commentaries and correct any wrong ideas you may have had. Ask yourself four questions about the passage: (1) What does it say? (2) What does it mean? (3) What does it mean to me? and (4) How can I make it meaningful to others? Do not bypass that third question! A sermon becomes a message when it is filtered through the heart and life of the preacher.

Organize your material. Clear preaching begins with clear thinking. You should be able to state your message in one concise sentence. Your main points should develop and support this one sentence or proposition. An outline is important; it helps people follow your message and remember it. It also helps you digest it so you can preach with freedom. Find that place where divine truth touches human life: that is where your message is.

Let the Lord use you. Sermon preparation is a spiritual experience. It can be compared with wrestling, or fighting a battle, or even the travail of a woman with child! The Spirit must speak *to* us before He can speak *through* us, so receive God's message first to your own heart: "What does this mean *to me?*"

Keep in contact with your people. There is no conflict between pastoring and preaching: they complement each other. As pastors, we get to know the needs of our people; as preachers we use the Word to meet these needs. Often you will find a message spring full-blown in your heart while ministering in a hospital room or standing at a new grave. The ivory tower preacher, who descends twice a week to deliver an oracle and then retreats into his sanctuary, may have great scholarship and homiletical excellence; but he will not have warmth and that personal touch. It will be the "sea of glass" *not* "mingled with fire." "Within the veil" and "without the camp": these two phrases from Hebrews describe the life of the faithful minister.

Keep alert! We are *always* preparing messages! Keep your eyes and ears open for illustrations, ideas, and new approaches. Jot down ideas in your pocket secretary or else you will forget them. Keep a sermon notebook or file and keep adding material to it. Andrew Blackwood called this the "sermonic seed-plot." You never can tell when some seed might blossom into a helpful sermon.

Each man must work out his own schedule. The old adage is right: "Plan your work and work your plan." And keep in mind that you are involved in eternal business that deserves the very best you can give.

How can I keep balance in my preaching so I don't end up riding some hobby that I especially enjoy?

Spurgeon told about the two farmers that met at the Monday morning market. "Did you go to church yesterday?" the one asked the other. "Yep," was the reply. "Well, what did you hear?" "Oh, the same old thing — ding-dong, ding-dong, ding-dong!" "You're fortunate," said his friend. "All we ever hear is ding-ding-ding-ding!"

Your own personal growth, through study and service, is the best way to assure your people a balanced diet from the Word. 2 Timothy 3:16 gives us "*all* Scripture" and Jesus said, "Man shall not live by bread alone, but by *every word* that proceedeth out of the mouth of God" (Mt 4:4, italics added). Keep digging into the Word and daring to pioneer into new territory, and you and your people will grow.

This is where expository preaching becomes valuable. The wealth of the Word makes its demands on those of us who preach it. You cannot play the music of heaven on one string! Let God direct you to a Bible book, and preach your way through that book, come what may. We suggest you select the book carefully, and read it through several times, before announcing a series. Otherwise you may begin to build and have to stop!

Major on the great themes of the Word and avoid like the plague clever sermons on obscure texts. Deliberately tackle passages that you have avoided or even feared. Plan your preaching so there is balance. A wise wife plans her menus, and a wise pastor plans his messages: Old Testament and New Testament, evangelism and edification, duty and privilege, history and prophecy, conviction and encouragement.

Just because one man can preach for ten years in Romans does not mean every man can do it. Early in his ministry, W. Graham Scroggie began a long series on Romans and saw his congregation dwindle. A note from one of his listeners convinced him that his plan was foolish; and ever after he stuck to short series. Spurgeon told about a man who preached for years in Hebrews. When he came to 13:22 — "suffer the word of exhortation" — Spurgeon commented, "They suffered!" There are those few gifted souls who can preach through a book, verse by verse and phrase by phrase, but unless we have those gifts, we had better concentrate on preaching paragraphs that take us through the book in a sensible length of time.

It is vital that the pastor know the spiritual needs of the flock and feed them accordingly. This is why pastoral visitation and personal counseling are important. Variety and vitality — an unbeatable combination!

Some people in my church think I am liberal be-

cause I sometimes refer to other translations of the Bible besides the King James Version. Many of our young couples and new Christians use modern translations and paraphrases. What should I do?

Don't criticize or belittle the beloved King James Version. Feel free to amplify its meanings and explain some of the archaic phrases, but never belittle it. Every translation has its strengths and weaknesses, and you accept a translation for its strengths and in spite of its weaknesses. If you are acquainted with the languages of the Bible, you can be fairly independent of translations, good and bad.

Take time to explain to the church how the Bible came to us. Explain what translation is all about. Perhaps a missionary involved in translation work can assist you. Why prepare up-to-date versions for the missionaries and still retain older versions at home? For most Christians, it is simply a matter of education, and this takes time. (We knew a dedicated church member who actually believed the Bible was written in Swedish!)

It is necessary to warn your people against popular translations that may not be accurate; but do so with kindness. Some translations and versions we use for reading, and others we use for study. Some are excellent for their treatment of Greek tenses, others for their scholarly notes. Some churches have conducted a Bible Study Fair, with the church young people manning booths that display various translations and aids to Bible study. The young people explain to the visitors the merits of the translations and the uses of the aids such as Bible dictionaries and concordances.

If the majority of your people use the King James Version, then use it yourself. If you sense there is need for a change, then work with your officers and plan the change carefully. Some churches have voted to put a modern version in the pews, and this has encouraged people to accept the change.

Often Sunday school classes are easier to influence than the entire church; but be careful not to split the church! And be sure that the version you adopt is really an improvement!

Don't make versions a test of fellowship. There are a few fussbudgets in almost every church who think one version or another is God's gift to man. Love them, be patient with them, and be thankful they read the Bible at all! That is more than many church members do!

6

THE PASTOR AND HIS BOOKS

What is the best way to organize my library?

The Dewey Decimal classification is standard and probably the best; but it can be time-consuming. Most pastors arrange their Bible study books in the scriptural order: (1) Old Testament introductions and surveys, (2) Genesis through Malachi, (3) intertestamental period, (4) New Testament introductions and surveys, (5) Matthew through Revelation. You can set aside special places for theology books, dictionaries and lexicons, biographical books, and sermons. Regardless of what approach you take, have a system and follow it.

Keep the books you use most often close to your desk or right on the desk: a Bible dictionary, an English dictionary, a Greek lexicon, a Hebrew lexicon, a handy concordance (both Strong's and Young's are happier open on a dictionary stand), and whatever other literary tools help you in your studies.

Keep a shelf handy near your desk to hold books relating to your current preaching plan. If you are going through the gospel of Mark, place all the commentaries on this shelf within easy reach. It is also wise to keep the standard commentaries you use close at hand. This saves a lot of up-and-down motion.

Be sure to index your library! Otherwise, you will never know what material is available. You need not index the commentaries since they are all in order on your shelves. But you will want to index sermons; special studies in miscellaneous books, such as the parables, miracles, names of Christ; and material in dictionaries and encyclopedias that you might overlook. *Baker's Textual and Topical Filing System* (Grand Rapids, Mich.: Baker, 1966), is very easy to use, and keeping it up-to-date will not require a full-time secretary. It is a large book with a simple number system that enables you to locate any item in your library in a minute's time.

You will probably want to file clippings and articles in manila folders. These, too, can be included in your topical filing system. Many pastors record illustrations on 3 by 5 cards and file them under key themes: redemption, giving, inspiration, et cetera. Be sure you write out all the necessary information so the illustration is clear and accurate. Nothing is more distressing than taking out an illustration card that reads "boy with dog in lake." Now, what *was* that all about?

Don't become a slave to a system. Keep your method simple and it will save you time. Don't feel that you must file away every clipping, and do plan to clean out the file regularly.

It is vital that your filing system include an index of sermon material in your library. Most sermon sets are indexed, such as G. Campbell Morgan's *Westminster Pulpit* (Westwood, N.J.: Revell, 1954) and Spurgeon's *Treasury of the Bible* (Grand Rapids, Mich.: Zondervan, 1966). But a master sermon index will enable you to locate any message on a given text or theme quickly. You can use three-by-five-inch cards if you wish, devoting one card to each Bible chapter. You need only list the verse, the volume and page number of the sermon, and it is done! The Baker system mentioned before handles this quite beautifully.

In one of his excellent books, Wilbur Smith suggests that the pastor index articles from Bible dictionaries and encyclopedias that might be overlooked. The average man would not remember that *The Dictionary of Christ and the Gospels* (New York: Scribner, 1907) has a great article in it on "Preaching Christ." Your index will remind you.

Index a book as soon as you get it, and mark on the inside cover "indexed." If you permit books to accumulate without indexing them, you will end up with a gargantuan task and probably decide the index is too much work and not worth it! In that direction lies ruin.

How large should my library be, and what books should it contain?

Size is no guarantee of quality. Better to have two hundred useful books than a thousand that only fill the shelves. The pastor cannot afford merely to be a collector of books; time money, and space are too precious — and an occasional move to another pastorate could make a man wish he never owned a book!

You want to build your library on tools and not crutches. A good book helps you study the Bible; it does not do the studying for you. "Sermon help" books are like TV dinners — good for an emergency, but not for a steady diet. You will need the best translations of the Bible, as well as lexicons and dictionaries to assist with the original languages. Your commentaries should reflect dedicated scholarship; they should tell you what the text *says* and what it *means*. Devotional commentaries are fine for devotional reading, or to "prime the pump," but they soon wear out when you start digging into the gold mine of God's Word. It is often by "digging again the old wells" and getting back to forgotten writers that we can improve our own preaching ministry today.

The pastor who wishes to build up his library with the better books should consult the bibliographies available. Dr. Wilbur M. Smith has written two excellent ones: *A Treasury of Books for Bible Study* (Natick, Maine: Wilde, 1960), and *Profitable Bible Study* (1951) reprinted by Baker Book House in 1971. Harish D. Merchant has edited *Encounter With Books,* "an annotated bibliography of 1600 books on Christianity, the arts and the humanities." It is published by Inter-Varsity (1970) and is heartily recommended to you, mainly because the titles were selected by sixty-seven specialists and not simply one or two avid readers. Beatrice Batson has compiled *A Reader's Guide To Religious Literature* (Chicago: Moody, 1968) which covers the "great religious writings" from the Middle Ages to the twentieth century. The emphasis here is not on Bible study books but rather on the great literature that deals with Christian themes — literature the pastor ought to know about personally. An older work, but still helpful, is Spurgeon's *Commenting and Commentaries* (Grand Rapids, Mich.: Kregel, 1954). Many of the books he recommends are out of print, but it is surprising how many of the titles he lists are still available, or have been recently reprinted. Even if you do not follow his suggestions, you will enjoy reading his pithy comments!

Books are like clothes: what fits one person's needs and style may not fit another person's at all. What we may consider the best books may turn out to be the worst books for you! However, generally speaking, most evangelical pastors would agree on the basic titles that ought to be in the preacher's library.

Many seminaries and Bible schools have bibliographies available; and often the leading Christian periodicals issue helpful bibliographies. A new bibliography under the authorship of Dr. Wilbur Smith, whose stature in the world of books is known and appreciated by all book-loving pastors is *The Minister in His Study* (Chicago: Moody, 1973).

One final suggestion: get to know the best authors and you will have an easier time finding the best books. Before you invest in a book sight unseen, borrow a copy from a friend, or see if it is in your local library. (If you borrow a copy, *be sure to return it!* Keeping borrowed books is the unpardonable sin of the ministry.) If you watch the book catalogs and keep up with the reviews in the best periodicals, you will gradually acquire a taste for the better books, and you will get to know which titles are really worth purchasing. If in doubt, ask someone who knows. Over the years you will develop special interests of your own, and will probably become somewhat expert in some field — prophecy, Bible biographies, or one special book of the Bible. You may decide to acquire every book you can find on the Lord's Prayer, or the words from the cross, or the life of Peter. Fine — but keep in mind that *collecting* books is not the same as *using* books, and it can be an expensive hobby!

Because all pastor's interests are not the same, and because there are some excellent bibliographies available, we will not give a listing here. In our own study of the Word, we have found the basic books to be helpful; and most of these are listed in the books cited above. However, we would warn the beginning preacher against purchasing a book simply because somebody important or well-known says he ought to. We have done this, only to discover that we have filled our shelves with useless material while emptying our pockets of needful currency. Now we look before we buy! We suggest that you do the same.

Of course, you will also want books relating to nonbiblical subjects, such as history, biography, and science. These will vary with the interests of the pastor.

A beggar stood at an intersection holding a hat in each hand. When he was asked, "Why two hats?" he replied, "Business is expanding." The pastor's learning must always be expanding. The Bible is God's truth, and no book can ever take its place. But the best writings of the best Christians and other scholars will help us in our studies into truth. Never be afraid of truth, for all truth ultimately must come from God. Phillips Brooks often reminded his people that "all truth intersects," since God is the source of all truth. No matter what area of truth we are studying, it must ultimately lead us to Christ who is the fulness of God's wisdom.

Again, beware of collecting books simply to fill the shelves. Purchase books carefully and build a library that is useful, not just decorative.

Books are expensive! How can a pastor purchase books when he has a limited budget?

God has promised to supply our needs. If a man's determination to be a good student is the real thing, God will see to it that he has the tools he needs. God does not provide luxuries, but He does supply needs.

Often, honoraria can be used for books. You and your wife should have an agreement about this. Sometimes it means real sacrifice on your part to get a much-needed book. When you buy books, you do not *spend* money — you *invest* it.

Many churches now have a book fund for the pastor. Some churches have even enrolled in book clubs and other money-saving plans to secure books for the pastor's library and for the church library. Of course, the books purchased for the pastor with this fund belong to the pastor, not to the church.

Watch for bargains in books: publisher's overstock sales, shopworn items, and special sales at conferences. Visit the secondhand stores in your area, the Goodwill Industries or Salvation Army. Often you will find excellent volumes at very low prices.

There are still a few used book outlets overseas. If you get on their mailing list, they send you lists of books regularly. Used books can come into the country duty free. If books you order are available, they will be sent to you with the invoice. *Pay your bill immediately!* We visited a London book shop and the manager showed us an embarrassing list of names of American pastors who owed him money. Brethren, such things ought not so to be!

Finally, *never buy a book you don't need simply because it is cheap!* A useless book is not a bargain; it is a thief.

What kind of reading should I do, apart from preparation for preaching and teaching?

Wide reading is valuable to a growing pastor. Everything you read can be used in your ministry. Bishop Quayle observed, "Every department of human thought must be the preacher's concern, solely because he is a man."

A man's interests and tastes will dictate much of his reading, but he must avoid reading the same kind of book over and over. By all means get a library card and use it! During your pastoral visitation, stop at the library for a quarter of an hour and browse among the books. Note the special shelves containing new listings. Most libraries issue regular bulletins with their new titles listed, so get on the mailing list. Read book reviews in your metropolitan papers and the better magazines, secular and religious.

Along with contemporary books, the pastor should read the newspaper and a good news magazine. All of them have their faults, so select those that do the most for you. Of course, you will want to read the best in religious journalism, too.

An ideal time to catch up on your magazine and newspaper reading is just before and after meals. Pastors who are privileged to have lunch at home with the wife can use part of their lunch period for relaxing reading (providing the wife does not have some crisis she wants to discuss). Ten or fifteen minutes devoted to reading before and after your evening meal will help both mind and body. It is amazing how much reading can be done when you invest short segments of time wisely.

Ask your pastor friends, and the good readers in your church, what they are reading. Often a recommended book becomes just the thing you were looking for.

While focusing on the contemporary, don't ignore the great books of the past. Wasn't it Mark Twain that defined a "classic" as "a book everybody talks about but nobody reads"? There are some books that we ought to read and know simply because they are permanent fixtures in American writing: books such as *Moby Dick, Walden, Pilgrim's Progress* (it is amazing how many pastors have never read Bunyan's classic!), and *The Scarlet Letter.* To go back even farther, what about the *Illiad* and *Odyssey,* Boswell's *Life of Johnson,* Benjamin Franklin's *Autobiography,* and a host of other classics? Many pastors take a classic along on vacation and read it. At first, their reading is a chore; and then the spell grips them and they say, "Is this what I have been missing all these years?"

A pastor cannot afford to be a "bookworm," but neither can he afford to ignore books. The secret is balance, and it may take you time to discover your own best schedule.

I am not the student type. I am more the active type. How can I discipline myself to be a better student?

When God calls, God equips and enables. God may not make you another Calvin, but He will help you fulfill your own potential. He will give you a love for the Word and a desire to study it and obey it. Not only do you need the Word for yourself, but you need it in order to feed your people. A careless ministry is a curse, and sorry is that congregation that must listen to a pastor who is unwilling to prepare himself and his messages.

What is "the student type" after all? Are you thinking of

an ivory-tower scholar who so lives in his books that he does not know what day it is? Then thank God you are *not* "the student type"! One of the qualifications for the pastor is "apt to teach" (1 Ti 3:2); and "apt to teach" involves "apt to learn." The Greek word here is *didaktikos;* it has come into the English language as didactic — "fitted to teach, instructive." We must be receivers if we would be transmitters. The pastor cannot afford to be like the spider, and spin everything out of his own mind; nor can he be like the ant, and steal morsels from others. He must be like the bee and gather nectar, but "make his own honey." (Bacon used this comparison; we borrowed it from him.) Or, to change the image, the pastor "milks a lot of cows, but he churns his own butter."

Scholarship is a stewardship; we will answer for the use of our time, abilities, education, and opportunities. With God's help, the pastor who hated Greek can learn to use and enjoy the basic tools of the language, and no doubt enrich his life and ministry. The more we do a thing, the easier it ought to become. Many pastors used to hate going visiting; but the more they visited, the more they enjoyed and appreciated it. So with studying: give yourself time to grow and hit your stride. But don't use the excuse, "I'm not the student type." There is no "student type." Paul's words are as true today as when he wrote them: "Study to shew thyself approved unto God, a workman that needeth not to be ashamed, rightly dividing the word of truth" (2 Ti 2:15). And while you are in 2 Timothy, take time to read 3:13-17.

To summarize: your own personal needs, the needs of your people, and the wickedness of this evil day all demand that we be the best students possible. The sword of the Spirit is as sharp as ever, but we must perfect our handling of it in the battle.

7

CHURCH SERVICES

How can I keep our services from being "the same thing" week after week?

Since the preacher is the same and the congregation usually the same, the only variety can come from the order and contents of the meetings. We have already discussed variety in your preaching. Try to have variety in the music as well. It is amazing how few hymns are actually learned and used from the average hymnal. Some churches use the midweek service for the learning of new songs, and then these songs are introduced in the Sunday ministry. To always have all hymns, or all gospel songs, or all contemporary music, would make the services tiresome. Variety and balance are important.

Beware of "canned speeches." The pastor should vary his way of welcoming visitors and giving the announcements. Many churches eliminate announcements completely and trust the people to use their bulletins. Other churches register the people and give the announcements before the service begins. An organ interlude follows, then the doxology.

Vary the order of the services, but don't become eccentric.

It is important that we permit our people to exercise the gifts of the Spirit, yet too often they are mere spectators at a religious program. Asking spiritual people to share in the services can be a great blessing. Also, use gifted leaders in the reading of the Scripture, but be sure they are prepared. It is most unwise to call on somebody a few minutes before the service.

Whether we like it or not, the morning service usually has a more worshipful atmosphere; the evening service is freer; and the midweek service the most informal of all. We know of no scriptural teaching that demands that it be this way, but this seems to be the way churches function. There ought to be spiritual unity and liberty in all the services, but the services should not all be structured in the same way. "Business as usual" eventually means "out of business!"

We like to keep the evening service bright and happy, with enthusiastic singing, special music, and preaching that is attractive and exciting. The midweek service deserves careful preparation, but don't structure it too tightly. Let the people respond to the Word as you teach it. Ask the congregation questions; let them share experiences. "The wind bloweth where it listeth."

Beware of programming spiritual effects. The church is no place for novelties. If you feel led to make drastic changes in the church's worship experience, then consult with your leaders and be sure it is done in God's time and in God's way. Attracting a group of turned on young people while you drive away the older people who built the church is hardly a wise plan. *Change for the sake of change is novelty; change for the sake of improvement is progress.*

The key is your own growing spiritual experience. If you are alive in the Spirit's fullness, it will show up in your leading of the public meetings. But please don't try to imitate some pastor you may admire. Be yourself and the Spirit will use you to do the job He has called you to do.

Must I always give a public invitation?

Always give the gospel and make it clear that people must trust Christ. Of course, there are more ways to respond to God's invitation than walking down an aisle; but the public invitation at the close of a meeting is a good way to do it. You need not sing for twenty minutes to give a valid invitation. Any Christian hymn or gospel song can be used for drawing the net. We have often preached primarily to believers and closed with a hymn of dedication, only to see unsaved people come to be saved. If you announce a closing hymn, then make it clear that this is an opportunity for decision.

After the singing has ended, point out that interested people may want to see you afterwards; and make yourself available. Not every baby is born in public. Often we have seen people come to Christ after the close of the meeting. Also, follow-up visits in the home can prove fruitful.

We need not apologize for giving an invitation, but neither should we use the response (or absence of response) as the test of the success of the service. The harvest is the end of the age, not at the end of the meeting. A public invitation is not necessarily a test of orthodoxy, but neither is the absence of an invitation (or a resistance to it on the part of the pastor) a special mark of spirituality.

Those of us who are ministering in city churches never know who is in the meeting or what the needs are. For all we know, some stranger may be present who is thinking of jumping off a bridge. A loving invitation could be used by God to bring him to Christ.

The thing that many people resent about an invitation is pressure. If the Spirit is not drawing the net, better that the invitation close. If the Spirit leads you to continue, then continue; but do not use human pressure to try to accomplish spiritual work.

Is there any future for the midweek service?

Of course there is — *if* the pastor works at it. Too many pastors treat the midweek service like a stepchild and fail to give it their best. If you prepare, this service can be a real spiritual oasis for your people in the midst of a difficult work-week. Major on inspiration and instruction, on encouragement and sharing, and your people will come.

Don't structure the midweek meeting like a Sunday service. Come with your songs picked out and your lesson prepared, but be open to the Spirit's leading. Create an atmosphere of joy and encouragement. Give people the opportunity to testify, to quote the Word, to sing favorites. Introduce the newer members, and the new converts, and give them opportunity to share. This hour in the middle of the week can become the most exciting hour of the church's ministry.

Watch out for sameness: the same people praying, the same order of service, the same emphasis week after week. Prepare encouraging Bible studies in a series. We have used: the prayers of the Bible, the fruit of the Spirit (take one different fruit each week), God's precious promises, great chapters of the Bible, book studies, character studies, and doctrinal studies. The possibilities are endless!

Make the hour a happy experience. Avoid scolding! If you must chasten the family, do so in love, and do it early in the meeting. Then build up to a thrilling spiritual climax and send them away rejoicing. Your people are fighting battles and they need the midweek fellowship to recharge their batteries. You will have better services on the Lord's Day if you concentrate on making the midweek service a time of encouragement.

How can we avoid the summer slump?

We see no reason why the summer weeks should be a time of relaxing our ministry and telling God we are all going on a vacation. To be sure, some of our people will be gone, but others will bring visiting relatives to the services; so there ought to be some kind of balance.

Psychologically, it is bad to talk about and expect a summer slump. If we announce one, it is sure to arrive — and it may last longer than the summer! Challenge the people to make the summer months count, and throw yourself into the program with dedicated zeal. Tell your people to enjoy their vacations and come home ready for work. It may take a few summers, but you can actually turn vacation time into harvest time.

Plan a special sermon series for the summer weeks. If you are to be gone, secure the best pulpit supply you can. Start promoting early so the people will know that the church will be in business all summer. In fact, since many other churches close down during the summer, you can actually reach many new people who are looking for a place to worship.

Make plans during the winter to use your college students when they return home; and put the teenagers to work with them. Many churches have profited from five-day clubs, which are simply miniature vacation Bible school programs held in somebody's back yard for the neighborhood children. If you live in a city, you can conduct these in various locations all summer long and reach souls for Christ and children for Sunday school. The day camp program is also effective. The children meet at church and are bussed each day to facilities for a full program of recreation and Bible lessons. It is somewhat of a mobile VBS.

People often have more time in the summer than in the winter, so plan ways to put them to work. Summer is a great time for fellowship and a great time for new members to meet old members.

Train your members how to witness while on vacation. Those who go camping might even carry enough material for a Sunday school class or a church service. More than one family has been used of God to bring a spiritual witness to a park, and do it in an acceptable way. When campers return home, ask them to share the experiences the Lord has given them.

We see the summer months as a great time to do special things with children, young people, and college students who are busy during the rest of the year. Make your plans in advance so they can include them on their calendar. It is not necessary to plan a circus to attract them, but do aim for variety and vitality. Make use of God's out-of-doors.

Just be sure you approach the summer with a positive attitude, and before long the church will catch the vision. Once we decide that nothing can be done, nothing will be done.

How can I make the observance of the Lord's Supper a meaningful experience to the church?

Too often, the Lord's Supper is tacked onto the end of the service, run through hurriedly, and looked upon as an intruder. Such shoddy treatment is inappropriate.

Prepare for the Lord's Supper. Arrange the service so that there is plenty of time for the ordinance. Choose the hymns carefully. Try to avoid long, needless announcements. (That is a good suggestion for *any* service!) Bring a message that focuses on Christ and the cross. In the Lord's Supper, we remember our Saviour, not our sins; so emphasize His love and grace. The attitude of the pastor goes a long way toward creating the right spiritual atmosphere for the Lord's Supper. If you are impatient or upset because your sermon time is shorter, the people will detect it.

Church practices vary as to the time of the Lord's Supper, and the frequency of observance. Perhaps you can suggest (at the proper time) that the church vary the time: Sunday morning the first Sunday of the quarter, Sunday evening the second month, and Wednesday evening the third month. (Shift-workers appreciate this kind of a schedule.) You will discover that the type of service will change from month to month. So often on Sunday mornings we have visitors and people who are not part of the church family, and this can affect the spiritual climate.

Some churches have arranged to commemorate Christ's death on an off night, with only the church family invited. This is frequently done during the Easter and Christmas seasons. An evening devoted completely to the Lord's Supper can be a high and holy experience.

Have you ever thought of having the Lord's Supper at the beginning of the service rather than at the end? This way the people are not worried about time, and you can adjust your message accordingly. There is one complication: visitors and people who do not want to participate cannot leave at the beginning as they can at the end. But if you handle the matter carefully, no one need be embarrassed.

Teach your people the meaning of the Lord's Supper. Prepare your own heart, and suggest to your deacons that they also prepare their hearts. Meet with them in advance for a season of prayer and confession. If your hearts are in tune with God and with one another, God will give a blessing.

8

ACTIVITIES AND PROGRAMS

How can I best minister to the youth of my church?

Start by loving them and not being afraid of them! For some reason, many pastors are scared of their young people. Perhaps it is because we have the idea that we must be youth experts in order to reach and help them. While there are some men to whom God has given a special gift for working with youth, this does not mean that the average pastor must sit on the sidelines.

Young people are looking for reality, so be a real person and not a phony. Above all, don't try to be an imitation teenager. Nothing will turn off your teens like a pastor who uses teenage jargon, dresses like a teen, and tries to act like a teen. Act like a mature adult and they will accept you; imitate them and they will turn you off.

Learn how to listen! Even when their criticisms are foolish and their ideas are odd, listen to them patiently and try to be positive. This does not mean we have to agree with them, but it does mean we disagree in a positive manner, accepting whatever good points we can. Often a young person will feel good just because he had a chance to get something off his chest! An open ear and an open heart will go a long way toward building a solid youth ministry in a church.

Pray for your young people by name. Some churches provide an up-to-date list of their young people for church officers and other leaders to use in their own daily prayer time. If you have sixty young people in your church, arrange the list so that you pray for five each day. You will be amazed at what God will do.

Let the teens participate in the planning and presenting of the program. Have definite goals and guidelines, but let them carry the ball while you and the sponsors coach from the bench. Try not to criticize in public; a private chat with a problem teen will accomplish a lot more.

Everything in the youth program must point toward spiritual ends. The local church will have a hard time competing with other programs when it comes to sports and other activities, but you can be sure there will be little competition when it comes to spiritual matters. Give your teens a practical knowledge of the Bible because they will not get it any other way. Teach them the Christian way to face and solve problems. Help them to understand and accept themselves. The church ought to create an exciting atmosphere in which teens can mature, discover and develop their gifts, and grow into balanced adults — physically, socially, intellectually, and spiritually.

Often the pastor must be the youth director until he can train sponsors to do the job. If so, don't look upon this time as wasted: it is *invested* in the future of the church. When you touch a young person, you touch a whole family! Ask God to give you a dedicated couple that can identify with youth and work with them. Don't be impatient; when the right ones come along, you will be glad you waited.

Keep your youth in mind when you prepare for the Lord's Day. It is good to remember them in the pastoral prayer. Be sure there is spiritual food in the messages for them. Try to keep up on what is going on at school, and be sure to give recognition when your teens achieve something special. Young people enjoy getting mail!

If your high school crowd seems impossible, minister to

them the best you can; but start working with the junior high group. It is better to "grow" yourself a group of dedicated teens. It will take two or three years, but it is worth it. Remember, too, that successful youth groups come and go; so don't be discouraged if next year's crop is not as dedicated as this year's. After graduation, your leaders take off and you have to start all over; so plan ahead. Be on the lookout for good leadership and keep some "Timothy teens" in training!

Try to plan youth programs well in advance. In fact, there is no reason why one month's programs should not be "in the works" while the next two months are being planned. "Brain storm" with the teens themselves and you will be amazed at the good ideas they will come up with! Variety is important: change the themes; change the locations; vary the participants; plan some surprises. During the summer, take advantage of the out-of-doors. If you *plan* your youth calendar, you will have fewer crises.

Don't be discouraged. Often the most heartbreaking fellow turns out to be a great pastor or missionary! And those impossible girls will one day be godly wives and mothers, serving faithfully in the church. Remember your own youth when you are tempted to blow up.

Build a growing library of materials that can be used for youth activities, but avoid canned programs that treat the teens like kindergarten children. They need resource materials, but not prepared speeches.

Finally, teach your young people how to win souls. Witnessing young people are growing young people. You will have fewer problems with teens who are concerned about reaching their friends for Christ. Teens who are excited about Christ will want to share Him with others, so give them the opportunities. As a steady stream of new Christians flow into the group, you will have fewer problems with cliques and finding enough participants.

Should the pastor teach a Sunday school class?

Some pastors should and some pastors should not.

In favor of the pastor teaching would be these considerations: (1) he knows the Word and should be "apt to teach"; (2) he can set the right example and show the other teachers how to do it; (3) he ought to have a keen interest in the success of the Sunday school, and teaching is one of the best ways to show this interest; (4) he has the time for visitation and the cultivation of a successful class; and (5) teaching a class is a great opportunity for soul-winning and making contacts with new families.

Now for the *negative*: (1) teaching a class can wear a man out and make that morning ser~ ~n a bit difficult; (2) when he leaves the church, he leaves a .acancy that might be difficult to fill; (3) teaching could rob him of time that ought to be spent on other church responsibilities; and (4) it is hard for other teachers to compete with the pastor, if he is a capable teacher at all.

Our vote is *for*: we think the pastor ought to teach a class if his health permits it. Most likely, he will teach an adult class, and others can profit from his ministry. We reproduce after our kind. There is no reason why the pastor's class should not be a source of future teachers in the Sunday school. The argument that other teachers cannot "compete" with the pastor is childish: nobody in a spiritual church is competing with anybody, unless it be the devil! The pastor's teaching ought to help raise the whole level of the school.

Is there danger that the pastor will use up all his material in a class and thus rob the church? Hardly! The Bible is full of spiritual riches, and if a man preached or taught forty times a week instead of four, he could not exhaust it. (He might exhaust himself!) Many pastors have found that the spadework done for a Sunday school class has unearthed treasures they could use in the pulpit. If a man is steadily digging into the Word, he will have no problem teaching a lesson, preaching two sermons, and leading a midweek service during the average week.

When you arrive on the field, give yourself time to locate the class God wants you to teach. If you take the class the former pastor taught, be sure everyone understands that this is temporary. You may discover a serious weakness in some area of the school: center your ministry there. Build up that area, find somebody to take it over, and then move to another area.

There should be no competition between being pastor and being a Sunday school teacher. Members of the classes might try to create problems ("We want to attend the *pastor's* class!") but these can be handled personally and with kindness. Some pastors like to teach an "auditorium class" that is composed of any and all adults who want to attend. This large class then becomes a feeder for the other departments. However, it can also become a magnet to draw people away who ought to be in other classes.

As a church increases in size, there is a greater need for the smaller groups, such as Sunday school classes. It is here that people get acquainted, discover their gifts, and really get to work for the Lord. Use your Sunday school to recruit and train adults, and you will probably reach the whole family. It is here that the pastor can have a very effective ministry.

How do I go about enforcing age limits in Sunday school classes and youth groups?

With difficulty!

For the most part, children and teenagers are no problem; it's the adult constituency that gives us the most trouble, particularly the young ladies who never grow old. There are two ways to alleviate the situation, but they may not solve the problem completely. One is to let a class "grow old" with the teacher, and the whole group stay together until it has to be divided. Some Sunday schools announce "reorganization" every three or four years. This is sort of a religious fruit basket upset but if done in the right spirit can help level the age divisions.

The second suggestion is an open class for adults, somewhat of a catchall for those who don't want to identify with a graded class. Sometimes the pastor's class — or the auditorium class — falls into this category.

The old black preacher hit the nail on the head: "Learn to cooperate with the inevitable!" You will have a difficult time trying to enforce strict age limits, and it is our conviction that too fine a division is not good for a growing Sunday school. After all, this is a volunteer group and nobody *has* to come. To regiment adults in the name of religious education might be a dangerous enterprise.

Many Sunday schools have had great success with adult electives. This program permits the adults to group themselves at least once a year on the basis of lesson interest and not age. But no matter how hard you work at it, you will still have some very fine adults whose theme song is "I Shall Not Be Moved." Learn to laugh it off and live with it without erasing the sensible guidelines that every organization needs if it is to prevent chaos.

How can I help improve the music ministry in the church?

Our good friend, Dr. J. Vernon McGee, once said, "When Satan fell, he landed in the choir loft!" One seminary professor called the music committee "the war department of the church." Alas, in some churches, this is true.

Let's begin with a basic principle: the music in the church ought to be the expression of the spiritual life of the church. Colossians 3:16 relates music to the ministry of the Word, the mutual edification of the church, and the condition of the believer's heart. In other words, if there is trouble with the music, the heart of the problem is the problem in the heart. The solution is not a new set of hymnals or an expensive new organ. The solution is a deep working of the Spirit in the hearts of the people. So, in your ministry of the Word, teach your people what it means to sing just as you must teach them what it means to pray.

Good Christians can disagree in their musical likes and dislikes, but all spiritually-minded people will agree on these propositions: the lyrics must be true to the Word, the tune must be wedded to the words so that one helps the other, and those who present the music must do so honestly from the heart. With the first, we have no problems: any Bible student can tell when a song is not true to Christian doctrine. (And, sad to say, we have plenty of them!) It is with the second that we have a real problem, because not every Christian knows when a hymn tune is really suited to the words. Tunes, like salads, appeal to different kinds of people. So, here we must exercise love and patience.

As to the third proposition, only the Lord (and the musician) knows whether the song is being presented in a sincere manner. The difference between ministry and performance is right here: ministry comes from the heart, performance from the mouth. Anyone who ministers in music publicly in a church should practice what he plays or sings. Anything less is hypocrisy. To summarize: the music in the church ought to be made up of fit words put to fit tunes, presented by spiritually fit people.

Congregational singing is something else. As the church grows in the Lord, it needs new expressions of its praise and faith. You cannot sing "Jesus Loves Me" forever. Use the midweek service to teach your people new songs. At first, some of them will resist this; but present the songs in such a spiritual way that they will be so blessed their resistance will stop. Tie each song to the Word of God. After they sing a hymn or gospel song, go over the lyrics line by line, and ask the congregation for Bible verses that relate to the words. This can be a thrilling experience for a church, and it will make the old hymnal a new book.

There are three keys to good church music: spirituality, balance, and excellence. Avoid music that moves the feet but not the heart. Music that appeals to the flesh can never be used to edify the spirit. Be sure there is variety and balance: too much of a good thing is as destructive as not enough. Keep in mind that your worshipers are at different stages in spiritual growth, and some of the "babes" have to express their faith, too. Finally, never settle for the mediocre. Aim for excellence. Not every church can afford a gifted music director, but the Spirit does give gifts to men, and He also brings gifted men to serve in the church. Pray for the kind of music director you need, whether a part-time layman or a full-time minister. And, *be patient!* Don't criticize the music publicly and embarrass people. Work behind the scenes to develop spirituality, balance, and excellence, and God will help you make changes at the right times.

How do we go about finding dependable missionaries to support?

Usually your denomination (if evangelical) has missionaries that need support. Avoid missionaries connected with "splinter" boards, the kind made up of the missionary, his wife, his father-in-law, and his great-aunt. You should have a missionary policy for the church that requires all workers to belong to *bona fide* boards that follow sound business practices such as auditing their books and sending out statements. Many churches require that the boards belong either to IFMA or EFMA. If the board is solid, the workers will usually be dependable.

Talk to other pastors. If you are considering a missionary, interview him personally, and get recommendations from his home church and from the churches that are supporting him. Watch out for missionaries who change boards or fields repeatedly. No missionary should ever be put on a church budget who has not been interviewed.

One area to watch is the recommendations of church members. Sad to say, some of the sheep are very gullible and believe everything they read in their third-class mail. Listen kindly to their ideas, but don't commit yourself. Never have a missionary in your pulpit who has not been recommended to you by another pastor or missionary whose judgment you trust. The fact that a member of your church is going to the field does not mean the church must give support. It is good to support our own members first, but each case must be handled individually. This is where a church missionary policy is valuable.

Try to have a balanced missionary program, at home and abroad. Some churches send all their money to Africa or Japan and forget that we were sent into *all* the world. Some support evangelistic works only and forget that national Christians also need hospital and educational institutions. Simply because a missionary is available does not mean we must support him. We must keep a total ministry in view.

My problem is that the church is so missionary minded they neglect the home base! What should I do?

Dr. Oswald Smith says it best: "The light that shines the farthest shines the brightest at home." The word used in Acts 1:8 is *and,* not *then.* When we move to "the uttermost part," we don't forget Jerusalem!

Prayer, patience, and preaching — that is the answer. Churches must be educated, and this takes time. Get busy winning people to Christ and teaching your people to witness, and before long a fire will start to burn at home. Set up a definite financial program for the home base and the missionary ministry. Remind your people that it is not a sin to spend money on buildings and supplies at home, because the money they send to the foreign field is spent on buildings and supplies!

Your own missionaries, when they return home, can be a great help here. Any missionary worth his salt knows that his work in the field is finished when the home churches fall apart.

In your public pastoral prayers, remember your missionaries by name, and try to cover all of them over a period of weeks; but pray for the work at home as well. Give recognition to work done well at home. Don't give your people the idea that God has a special reward for Christians with passports. In time, the attitudes will change, and you will be able to build the home base as well as the missionary ministry.

To what extent should the local church be involved in welfare or social work? Is this really a part of the gospel?

Jesus went about doing good (Ac 10:38). The early church helped people in need. The Old Testament prophets thundered against the selfishness of God's people because they failed to care for the needy. We are commanded to "do good unto all men, especially unto them who are of the household of faith" (Gal 6:10).

The problem is that too many churches substitute good deeds for the witness of the gospel. It is not a matter of either/or but both/and. Helping men with their physical and material needs is in itself a ministry (Heb 13:16); and it also prepares the way for a further ministry of Christian witness. We must prove to people that we care, before they will believe that

God cares. And, if it is right to minister in material ways on the mission field, why is it wrong at home?

Of course, the local church must not abandon the gospel for social work. But there are people in every church who can visit needy homes, help supply food and clothing, assist men and women in finding jobs, and in a hundred ways share the love of Christ. If Acts 6 is any indication, this work ought to be in the hands of the deacons and their wives (or deaconnesses, if your church has them).

It is usually unwise to hand people money out of your fellowship fund. It is better to help them purchase what they need. Many churches keep their fellowship fund supplied by receiving a special offering after the communion service. Other churches simply vote a designated amount to be distributed by the pastor and deacons.

Somebody on your staff should get acquainted with the welfare agencies in your city. It is usually best to check with them before going too far in helping a family. Unfortunately, some needy people go from church to church and rob the saints. We have known of families with several children who "farmed out" the children into various churches and Sunday schools, especially around Christmas and Thanksgiving, and in this way reaped a bountiful harvest. Most agencies are only too happy to cooperate with you and share whatever information they can.

While we are on this subject, please educate your church family *not* to send useless castaway clothing and utensils to the missionaries. The philosophy of some Christians seems to be, "It's no good to us, so now it's good enough for the missionaries!" Shame on us! We have even been told of church members sending *used tea bags* to the field! Our missionaries deserve the best, not the worst.

How can we determine whether or not the church should go into a building program?

At least four factors are involved: need, the spiritual condition of the people, resources, and future plans.

If the work is prospering, you will need more space in which to operate. Try to get the maximum use of your space before you start to build. Some churches conduct split Sunday schools and are quite successful. Preaching at two morning services is a chore, but it is being done. Of course, if the condition of the building(s) is bad, you will have to do something. Watch the growth of the work; keep accurate statistics. Before long, you will know if a definite need exists.

To build without discerning the spiritual condition of the people is to court trouble. A building program is difficult enough when the church is spiritual; it would be disastrous with a carnal congregation! It is usually unwise to suddenly spring a program on your people. Start with the leaders of the church. Spend time in prayer and consultation. Try to take the pulse of the church. Are we united? Do we see evidence of spiritual growth? Have we the faith to move ahead? Is our stewardship evidence that we trust God and obey the Word? To be sure, you will never have one hundred percent on all these matters, but you had better have more than fifty percent. The success or failure of any matter involves careful timing, and in no enterprise is it more true than a church building program.

Your financial resources are important. Every cloud has a silver lining, but it is sometimes difficult to get it to the bank! Nothing strangles a church like an impossible debt. A sensible debt is a stimulus to faith and sacrifice, but an impossible debt puts the church under a dark cloud of gloom. You will always have the doubters who see a depression around the corner, or bankruptcy, or the ruin of the church. These people we love, pray for, and try not to take too seriously. But "in the multitude of counselors there is safety." Evaluate your situation; investigate your resources; let God give you wisdom and discernment.

Finally, never build without a definite plan for the future. Better to delay building for a year while you draw up a total program than to cripple future expansion because of a hastily built structure. We never build just to impress people, or to relieve a pressing situation. We build because we have a total program for the expansion of the work, and this step is a part of that program.

There are several church building consultants, men of real evangelical faith, who are available to help in these matters. It may cost the church a few extra dollars to secure their services, but the investment will save time, money, and trouble in years to come. It is amazing how many church members who know nothing about engineering suddenly become experts when a building program gets underway! Our Lord's parable about the basement building can be applied in more than one way (Lk 14:28-30).

9

VISITATION

How can I have a successful ministry of pastoral visitation?

If we expect our people to engage in visitation, we must set the example ourselves. Furthermore, if our preaching is to touch the real needs that people have, we must, like Ezekiel, "sit where they sit." So, begin by realizing the importance of pastoral visitation. You cannot win souls or shepherd the flock simply by sitting behind a desk or standing behind a pulpit. Read James 1:27 if you have any doubts as to the value of a visit; then read Matthew 25:36 and 43.

Let's start with pastoral visitation among your own people. Set aside definite stated times during the week when you will visit the hospitals. Of course, the amount of time needed depends on the size of your locality and the number of hospitals involved. Unless a patient is very ill, it is not necessary to visit him daily. If you have staff assistants, share the hospital calling with them by giving each one a specific day. Keep a hospital list in the church office with all necessary information. After visiting, the pastor can add whatever facts he thinks are necessary. Be sure to mark when the patient has gone home so no other staff member will waste time making a call. File the "hospital calling sheets" for future reference.

Some churches are smaller and the pastor can call in every home in a month or two and then start over again. Others demand more time. Never call in a home just to be calling.

Always have a stated purpose: to get better acquainted with the family; to share some spiritual blessing; or to discuss some vital matter. Visits need not be long, and do resist the urge to enjoy coffee and cake in every home.

A card file or notebook should suffice to keep a record of the calls made. Arrange your calls geographically as much as possible; it will save you time. Also, when returning home from funerals, plan to make some visits if possible on the members who live on the "fringes of the camp."

You should build a list of prospects and unsaved people and keep working at it. There are people in the community, particularly men, who will respond to the witness of a concerned pastor. Some pastors set aside one special time a week just to go soul-winning. This is a thrilling experience and really helps stoke the fire for Sunday's preaching!

As much as possible, let your Sunday school teachers and church members visit the new prospects and the people who visit church services. If they feel a contact is encouraging, they can let you know and you can follow through. But remember that, when the pastor visits, he is looked upon as a paid salesman. When a member visits a home, he is looked upon as a satisfied customer! Visiting, witnessing laymen who know how to win souls can bring power to a church, so take a man with you when you visit and teach him how to do it.

Most churches use a Sunday registration system for getting the names of visitors. This works much better than the visitors' book in the narthex.

Don't be discouraged when your visits seem wasted. You are serving God and obeying His Word whether people appreciate the visits or not. It often takes a dozen or more visits before a family will become interested. "In due season we shall reap, if we faint not."

Sunday school calling and religious surveys are programs by themselves. Many churches go out once a week to visit prospects and absentees; some go every other week or even once a month. The important thing is to set up a challenging program that meets the needs of your church. Simply to imitate another church's program because it is successful may be disastrous.

When making your pastoral visits, have a definite purpose in mind. Be a blessing, but don't waste time. Be spiritually sensitive to the atmosphere in the home. Never give the impression you are in a hurry, even though you may be; keep in mind that you are laying a foundation for future visits.

What suggestions do you have for hospital visitation?

Get to know the hospital personnel and make yourself available to help them; but don't assume authority that you don't possess. If there is a chaplain in charge, by all means become his friend, even if you are of different faiths.

Visit at hours convenient to the patients. Many pastors find that late morning, after baths and bed changes, is a good time for the patients: they are fresh and clean, they have not been worn out by other visitors, and there will be fewer interruptions. Arrange your visits according to the rules of the hospital; don't write your own rules. Pastors are usually permitted to visit at any time (except in the maternity ward), but don't make a pest of yourself. One pastor visited at 11:00 P.M. and fell asleep praying for the sleeping patient!

Be cheerful! Leave *your* problems and symptoms outside the door and enter the room determined to be an encouragement.

Remain a pastor; don't become an amateur physician. It is wrong to diagnose the case or to compare the patient with others you have met. Never act as go-between when the patient and his physician have a difference. You may not agree with the physician in charge, but you should not argue with him.

If the patient has fears or frustrations, be a counselor and help him find peace in Christ.

Be brief. Long visits (unless you are really doing spiritual business and the patient insists you stay) can often do more harm than good. Each visit should help to lift the patient with hopefulness and joy.

In most cases, read something brief from the Word and pray to the point. Don't turn the bed into a pulpit and preach to the whole ward "over God's shoulder." A quiet, personal prayer at the bedside is what the patient needs.

Pay attention to the others in the room; greet them and be friendly. If it is a double room, or three-bed room, be sure to include the other patients in your prayer. If they are visiting with others, wait for a break in the conversation and ask, "Would you mind if I prayed for all of us?" Very few patients or visitors would be offended. Often the patient's names are on cards over the beds, so you can mention them by name as you pray. Many pastors have won people to Christ simply by being kind to them in the hospital while visiting another patient!

Use Christian literature judiciously. Be sure to read carefully whatever you distribute; the wrong tract can do untold damage.

As much as possible, get the facts about the patient. One pastor asked a patient, "Was this an emergency, or did you plan to come in?" The patient replied, "Oh, I planned to come in. I just had a baby!" Because she was not in the maternity ward, due to hospital remodeling, the pastor was caught by surprise. A minute at the desk would have saved him embarrassment.

Tell the lost about the Saviour. Do it with kindness and love. Better to share the Word when you have the opportunity than to lose a soul while waiting for a better opportunity.

It is wise to train your people in the best ways to be a blessing while visiting in the hospital. Often in messages or prayer meeting fellowships, we have opportunity to warn against deathbed stories, home remedies, loud talking and praying, and the other horrible practices that often make Christians unwelcome in the hospital. In fact, some church members should be advised not to do hospital visitation at all! They may not like it, but better to upset a few saints than to lose your testimony in a whole hospital.

How can I encourage our members to visit?

By example, first of all. Visiting is better *caught* than *taught*. It spreads best by *contagion,* not *compulsion.*

Start with a few choice men; your wife can encouarge the women. Take them with you when you visit. Ask God to touch their hearts. Once they have learned the approach, and experienced the blessing, they can share it with others. In a few years, you can multiply yourself.

Courses taught on visitation and soul-winning are valuable *if* they include on-the-spot experience with people who know how to visit. Our members can pass courses on witnessing and never witness! One lady told her pastor, "I have taken four courses in soul-winning, and yet I have never tried to win a single soul to Christ."

At the right point in your ministry, God will burden you to preach on the *going* aspect of the church's ministry. The book of Acts is full of it! Emphasize the *why* and *how* as much as the *what.* Unless the Holy Spirit is in charge, our activities will become just more busy work in an already overloaded church program.

Give opportunities for your people to testify of the blessing of visiting. But warn them not to scold the people who don't share in this ministry. Some of your people should not call, but they can pray for those who do call. Beware lest your busy group of callers become a "spiritual elite" in the church, with a "holier than thou" attitude.

Prepare attractive literature about the church and its ministry so your people will have ammunition to use during the week. *Never* put negative, critical items in the Sunday bulletin, since this can be used the wrong way. A bright bulletin is a good promotional piece; a sloppy one is better not printed at all.

One more thing: as pastor, be sure that the ministry is worth inviting others to share! The best encouragement you can give your people in this matter of sharing Christ is a ministry of the Word that they can enthusiastically invite people to attend. And keep in mind that, though your members bring in the visitors, it is primarily the pastor's job to keep them coming!

How should we recognize visitors in the services, and what is the best way to follow up their visits?

This depends on the size of your congregation. It is a basic rule that no visitor should be embarrassed or put on display. Some people are sensitive and would resent public recognition. In smaller churches, the pastor often sees who is visiting because he knows his congregation so well.

The guest register in the narthex is often ignored as people come and go. It is better to ask *all* the people to register each week, and in this way the visitors are not singled out. Some churches ask the visitors to lift their hands, and they are given a registration card and souvenir packet of materials. The cards are collected during the offering or at the close of the announcements.

The effectiveness of a visitors' recognition time depends on the attitude of the pastor. If he is the friendly type, he will make the visitors feel at home. If he is reserved, perhaps it would be better if some other man did the recognizing. Perhaps the deacons could share the ministry.

Some churches have a visitors' reception immediately after

the morning service, with light refreshments; and here the pastor and his wife can meet all the visitors at one time. It is easier to get them to sign the guest book in a reception, by the way. Each week have different members of the church present as greeters and mixers.

On Monday morning, either a postcard (prepared exclusively for your church) or a letter should go out to each visitor. Keep the registration card for future use. Perhaps some member of the church could volunteer to serve as director of this follow-up ministry, keeping the records and mailing materials. Since the person has visited you, it is proper to return the visit. In most cases, it is better for church members to return the visit rather than pastor, lest other pastors think he is out to "steal their sheep." During the week, someone from the church should visit the home to thank them for their visit and to determine what the future holds. If the people are active in another evangelical church, simply thank them for visiting. If they are looking for a new church home, or if there are spiritual needs in the home, this should be communicated to the pastor.

We believe we owe it to our fellow pastors to let them know if some of their sheep are visiting around. Sometimes there are church problems that you don't want to invite into your church! This does not mean that church members have no right to relocate, but such moving should be done in the right spirit. The visitor who criticizes his pastor will criticize you when he joins your church, so go easy on trying to build with borrowed bricks.

10

MARRIAGE AND DIVORCE

How can I best prepare young couples for marriage?

There are two kinds of preparation: the general kind that is the result of your own life and your ministry of the Word; and the specific kind for couples planning to get married.

The preacher who expounds the Word is bound to cover many themes relating to the Christian home. Note in Ephesians and Colossians how Paul writes to husbands and wives, and even to the children. Jesus had much to say about family living, and the Old Testament writers deal with the topic, too. Once a year you may want to do a special series on the home, but don't make it too long or too negative.

Be sure that the people who direct your youth ministry give proper place to marriage and the home. The time to prepare husbands and wives is in their maturing years when the material is still pliable.

There should be a good section on the Christian home in your church library. You ought to have several copies of the best books available, and make it possible for members to purchase their own copies. Occasional films will also help. Many churches have an annual seminar on the home, with a guest specialist invited in to lead the discussions.

Your specific ministry to a couple should begin as early as possible. When you see that a couple have started dating steadily, let them know you are interested and would be happy to chat with them. God will give you direction here, so wait for His leading. Otherwise, the couple may think you are meddling. Set up a series of appointments with engaged couples, and don't complain about the time that it will involve! Better to invest your time *before* they are married than to have to invest more time after the marriage falls apart.

Several publishers have prepared special marriage inventory programs that the pastor can use in his counseling. Many denominations have excellent inexpensive books that can be used as the basis for a series of sessions. It is also wise to suggest that the couple visit their family doctor as soon as possible to talk with him about the physical aspects of marriage. There are several excellent books available on this subject, written by Christians, and these should be made available to the couple.

Don't assume that, because the couple grew up in the church and has always given evidence of spiritual life, that they will automatically have a successful marriage. Just about every church has experienced its heartaches when the "ideal young couple" got a divorce. If you detect any problems (and the marriage inventory helps here), deal with them honestly and lovingly. If you feel there is need for additional counsel, perhaps from a professional Christian counselor, then suggest that the couple get it as soon as possible. Marriage does not create problems: it reveals them. The time to solve them is before the couple says "I do."

The pastor does not have to marry anybody, but he must not feel that his decision is God's decision. We have ministered long enough to see some marriages that we questioned turn out to be very happy ones, and others that we thought were ideal turn out to be tragedies. It is difficult to make predictions in a matter so intimate as marriage. If you have serious reservations, discuss them with the couple in a frank but tender manner. Pray with them. Encourage them to seek God's guidance and help.

You will probably have your share of "crisis weddings," and you must take each one individually. Let your church know that you do not marry people without first counseling them. You may have some opposition here, but ride it out and stick to your position. When emergencies arise, consider the situation carefully and do what God leads you to do. We are dealing with human beings, not checkers on a board. Some marriages that today seem impossible will tomorrow bring joy to your heart. In some cases, your counseling will have to be after the ceremony instead of before; but this is better than no counseling at all.

Needless to say, your own home will help prepare couples for marriage, so open it up to the dating crowd and let them see a happy Christian family in action. And, the way you treat your wife and children in public will have an influence on others. When your "marriageables" see you setting the right example, they will be happy to listen to your counsel.

Divorce and remarriage seem to be controversial issues in many churches. How can I make the right decision on this matter?

Many good and godly men disagree on whether or not divorce and remarriage are scriptural, and the last word probably will not be said this side of heaven. The best thing for you to do is to examine the biblical teaching carefully and read widely on every position. Ask the Spirit to guide you, and don't be afraid of whatever truth the Lord reveals. "Let every man be fully persuaded in his own mind." Once you have adopted a position, try to stick to it in love. Avail yourself of the many books dealing with this topic, some of them by very fine scholars.

Beware of developing a "holier than thou" attitude toward people in the church who have had unfortunate marriages.

It is possible to be loving and understanding even if you disagree with people.

You will find it best to judge each case individually on its own merits. We believe that God forgives all manner of sin (Mt. 12:31), and that when God receives a person, we should receive him (Ro 15:7). To preach grace and practice law is inconsistent, and to make divorce and remarriage "unpardonable sins" is cruel. This does not mean that the church should lower its standards and cease to exalt Christian marriage, but it does mean we don't go beyond the Word in deal-with these matters. The pastor who stays in one church for any length of time is surprised almost every year to discover more cases of past marital mixups!

If a pastor feels that divorce is unscriptural or that remarriage after divorce (for any reason) is unscriptural and insists that couples involved should not be allowed in the church membership, then he must be consistent by dismissing from the church roll any who violate this position and refusing to accept into the church family all who violate it. We know of no scriptural precedent for such a position, and we wonder how it could be held in the light of 2 Corinthians 5:17, Ephesians 4:32, and dozens of other verses that clearly teach forgiveness and acceptance in Christ.

It is unwise for a pastor to marry strangers who are "passing through town." When they phone, let them know you prefer to counsel with people first. Not all states list the person's marital status on the license, and you might be performing a marriage out of the will of God. By the way, it is also unwise and unethical to send couples over to a brother pastor. You put that pastor in an embarrassing position.

Jesus came to "heal the brokenhearted" and that should be our ministry as well. We are going to see more and more marital problems in the days to come, and the answer is not stricter laws or tougher church membership procedures. The answer is a positive ministry to prepare our young people for maturity, and a compassionate understanding for those who have suffered. The church family is made up of all kinds of people (1 Co 6:9-11, Gal 3:28), and the pastor must love all of them and minister to all of them. Love, patience, prayer, the Word, and a practice of Ephesians 4:32 will go a long way toward mending broken hearts and broken homes.

You owe it to your church to share your convictions before accepting their call. It is our belief that the pastor should have complete freedom when it comes to marrying people, and that he should not be dictated to by a board or a congregation. There are situations that only he and the Lord should know about, and to answer to a board would be to violate confidence. To make views of marriage and divorce a test of fellowship or ministry is, to us, a most unfortunate thing. "We know in part."

What about young couples who *have* to get married?

Your first responsibility, as we see it, is to help the couple spiritually and minister to the other loved ones involved. This problem is more prevalent now and yet does not create the same stigma that it did a generation or so ago. As soon as you discover the problem, meet privately with the couple. Seek to lead them into God's forgiveness and acceptance.

Should they get married? If they already had planned on marriage and are suited for each other, then they ought to become man and wife. *But they should not marry simply because the girl is pregnant.* They should get married only if this is God's will for their lives. Often the very presence of the problem indicates that they should *not* get married, that something is radically wrong in their relationship. For them to marry just to give the baby a home, and then eventually divorce, would be adding sin to sin.

If they do not marry, they must decide on the future of the

child. Most communities have agencies for the handling of these babies, and you ought to help the girl to contact such an agency. She must make the decision, of course, but you can assist her in facing and solving the problems involved. Some girls want to keep the baby as a form of self-punishment, which creates a difficult situation for the child. In most cases, it is best to arrange to have the baby adopted into a Christian home where it is wanted. Then the girl can return to life and make a new beginning. Each case is individual, so we dare not make generalizations for every case.

If the couple, or either one of the two, is a member of the church, you should guide them into an experience of forgiveness on the part of the fellowship. Again, it is not necessary to display dirty wash, but neither should we make light of sin. It has been our experience that the young people of the church will know about the problem before many of the deacons discover it! If the member is unwilling to make things right, you will have to consider church discipline.

11

DEATH AND FUNERALS

How can I improve my ministry to the sorrowing?

Begin by making it the "law of the Medes and the Persians" that nobody will ever joke about death or tell funeral jokes in the public meetings of the church. We have seen some of our people completely crushed when a guest speaker tried to liven up the service by telling a joke about a funeral. People with broken hearts come to church for comfort and encouragement, not to have their hearts broken again.

The man with a pastor's heart will instinctively do the right thing when his sheep are "going through the valley." As soon as you hear of a death in a church home, try to contact the family. Perhaps you should phone first and see if a visit is in order. It is usually best to get to the home as soon as possible, no matter what hour of the day or night. We may set hours for counseling people but not for comforting people.

In the home, try to have a quiet ministry. A talkative, loud pastor is going to do more harm than good. Don't take over the family. After you arrive, express your sympathy, and stand by to listen and to help. Your visit need not be long. At some proper time in the visit, offer to read Scripture and pray; *and please do this with heart!* A perfunctory reading of the Word, followed by a routine prayer, will only make the wounds hurt more. Ask God to give you a heart of compassion.

Try to be at the funeral home before the family arrives for that first viewing. This is the crucial time, and the presence of the man of God will help the whole family. Walk into the chapel with them, and stand with them silently. Your presence is a sermon; there is no need to preach. Watch for indications of family tensions or problems; see how the people are responding to the death of the loved one. Half an hour devoted to the family at this point will give you a great deal of insight as you prepare the funeral message, and as you minister in the home in later days.

Plan the funeral service to meet the needs of the mourners. The closest relative to the deceased should have the final decision about time, place, music, et cetera. Ask whether there is any favorite Scripture that should be read. If you have been in the church a long time, you will already know the ins and outs of the family, and your preparation will be simpler. Keep the service brief and to the point; long services often make deeper wounds. Your message should focus on *one comforting truth;* this is no time for a doctrinal exegesis on death or resurrection. You are applying balm to broken hearts, so be tender.

Try to follow-up with a visit in the home as soon as possible. Watch for signs of emotional problems. You ought to read widely in the excellent literature available today on the psychology of grief. Be available to the mourners during these difficult days of adjustment. Also, be alert to family disagreements. Bereavement has a way of opening up old wounds, or of making people feel guilty. This is why there are often family fights at funerals!

Your whole pastoral ministry is helping to prepare people for the hour of sorrow. Preach as a dying man to dying men, and when death does come, both you and your people will be prepared.

Should I accept an honorarium for preaching at a funeral?

Most funeral directors write the honorarium into the total cost of the funeral. Some, however, leave it to the family. It is not wrong to receive an honorarium for services rendered; it is wrong to ask for one. If the family involved is not a part of your church, they certainly ought to pay you for taking time from your own people to assist them. Since most church members help to pay our salaries, accepting a gift from them is another matter. However, you will find that most church members *want* to show love and appreciation to their pastor in return for his faithful ministry to them. Do not be embarrassed: it takes grace to be a good receiver as well as a good giver. Just say, "Thank you. I'll use this in the Lord's work in some way." Many pastors invest funeral honoraria in books, and even write on the flyleaf, "A gift of the _____ family."

There are times, however, when accepting a gift would be unwise. At such times, suggest that the family put the gift into the church ministry as a memorial, or that they share it with a missionary cause. If they insist that you take it, do so, but give it to the church and send them a thank you note with a receipt. Church memorial gifts are being accepted more and more.

How do I minister to total strangers who ask me to conduct a funeral service?

Usually the funeral director calls and makes the arrangements. Get the necessary information from him, including any insights he has that will help you in your ministry. After you have been in a church a few years, you will find that most funeral directors are very anxious to help you.

Visit the home and get to know the people. Perhaps there are members in your church who know them, but beware of of prejudiced opinions from outsiders. When you arrive at the funeral home, watch for signals that will help you better understand the situation.

Obviously, a funeral message for a stranger cannot be as personal as one for a friend. Deal with the great truths of the gospel: don't preach the deceased into heaven or hell. Preach to the living. Your gracious handling of the funeral service should give you opportunity to minister to the family later and perhaps reach them for Christ and the church.

Should I use the same funeral messages over again? How can I develop new messages?

You will no doubt use the same passages or texts, but you will adapt them to the needs of the hour. Keep a notebook of your messages, and write on each sheet the data for each time the message was used. Ask God to give you a personal word for each service. To dig out an old message while driving to the funeral home is a sin. It is also a sin to repeat a routine message funeral after funeral. Each funeral is different, and each one demands a personal touch.

In your devotional reading of the Bible, you will come upon texts that will shout at you, "Preach me!" Add these to your notebook or sermon file (Andrew W. Blackwood called it the "sermonic seed-plot"), and let the Spirit mature the text into a message. If a man is walking with God, he will always have that "Word in season" from the Spirit (Is 50:4). As you grow in your own spiritual life, you will drop some messages and prepare many new ones. Some texts will be especially meaningful to you, and you will use them often.

This may sound morbid, but if you have elderly people in your church, hospitalized, or with terminal illnesses, ask God to give you just the message their loved ones will need, and be prepared before the person dies. There is no need to be in a panic if the person has been lingering for weeks. We would not tell our people that we have funeral messages prepared for them! But we would plan in advance. This especially holds true of the "pillars" in the church and the faithful officers who have labored long and hard. Newspaper offices have their prepared obituaries for great people; pastors can have sermon ideas maturing for their people.

12

FELLOW LABORERS

What should be my relationship to former pastors of the church, especially my immediate predecessor?

Stories about former pastors are often like stories about mothers-in-law: they are only stories. Make up your mind that you will not become jealous of any other servant of God, and that you will never consider a former pastor a threat to you or your ministry. It sometimes takes much grace to achieve this, but it is absolutely essential that you succeed.

To begin with, keep in mind that there is no competition in the Lord's work: we are all laborers together with God. No two men have the same gifts; no two men achieve the same goals; but God can call and use both men. One man plows, another sows, another waters, another harvests, but it is God that gives the increase (1 Co 3:3-9). So, your first step toward getting along with your predecessor is *a clear understanding of the meaning of the ministry.* He has his gifts and (we trust) has used them to make his contribution to the church. You have your gifts and will use them to build the church even more. The next man will come and make his unique contribution.

Always say something good about your predecessors. When members praise them, encourage their praise. Even if your predecessor was a failure in some areas (and aren't we all?), find something good to say about him. Do this sincerely, and not as a gimmick to make friends and influence people. If you are praying for him as you ought to be, you will have no problems.

When you hear criticism, try to cover it with love and kindness. The member who criticizes his former pastor will likely criticize you when you leave. Let the word get around that you will not tolerate unjust criticism. After awhile, it will probably stop.

Make friends with your predecessor if at all possible. If he is a man of God, he will not invade your field, visit your people, and deliberately cause trouble. But you cannot help but expect him to want to see the people if he visits the area, especially if they loved one another. Professional ethics would demand that he contact you first, but not all pastors know about ethics. Each pastor will have two or three families in the church with whom he was especially friendly; no good can come from trying to break up these friendships. Trust him not to cause problems. He should be wise enough not to visit the field too soon after you arrive, unless invited by the church. If he suggests visiting too soon, don't hesitate to tell him you would rather he wait. Openness and love usually prevail among men who walk with God.

The former pastor can be of help to you, but don't run to him with all your problems. Some of these problems he may have helped to cause himself! Furthermore, you don't want to start your ministry adopting his prejudices and viewpoints. Getting a run-down on all the members of the church could be the worst thing to happen to a new pastor! If this pastoral gossip starts, lovingly suggest that it not continue. This does not mean he cannot warn you about serious troublemakers (2 Ti 4:14-15), but it does mean that he refrain from sharing his likes and dislikes.

What about the older pastor who retires and stays on the field? This is a special situation and it requires an extra measure of grace. If he had a long ministry, he must be a good man in many ways, and the people must love him.

Share this love. Minister to your older brother in love and kindness and he will be a help to you. Also, your love for him will help to win the love of the church family. The instant any jealousy or friction appears, take it to the Lord and get it settled. Otherwise your whole ministry will be poisoned and the only result can be disaster. If the people prefer him for weddings and funerals, just be patient. Suggest that you open the service, or share some other way; but be willing for him to serve. In due time you will win the love and respect of your people and the problem will be solved.

When the right opportunity comes along, invite your predecessor to come back to preach. But keep in mind that not everyone will agree with this idea, because he will have left behind enemies as well as friends. Make it a happy occasion of homecoming and you will reap benefits in the years to come.

What do we do when the pastor left under a dark cloud? Quietly investigate the situation and come to your own conclusion. You have every right to talk to your predecessor and get his point of view. If there was a serious breach of morals, then you must be cautious in relating to him lest you open up old church wounds. You can certainly be a friend and Christian brother, but this does not mean you will necessarily invite him back or encourage the people to reopen the case. He will be happy if you just let the dust lie.

Some day, *you* will be a former pastor, so be careful how you act today. It is not easy, particularly if your successor seems to be tearing down what you worked so hard to build up. Leave it with God; don't meddle; don't write letters and gossip. Sometimes God gives a church just what they deserve!

What suggestions do you have concerning evangelists and special speakers: how to choose them, where to put them, how to handle finances, and so forth?

It is best to use men you have heard and that have been recommended to you by believers you can trust. Contact pastors who have used the man, and see what kind of work was done. Get your facts from life, not from the news releases.

When you invite a man in, get all the details settled in advance. Your church should cover his expenses to the meeting and during the time he is conducting the meeting. These expenses should not come out of the love offering. They should either be written into the church budget or taken care of by a special expense offering. It is unfair to the speaker to make him pay his own expenses out of his offering. Be sure that you have all the financial arrangements clearly worked out before the man arrives.

It is wise to put the speaker in a hotel or motel where he can have privacy. It may cost a few dollars more, but you will benefit from the investment. If you have ever had to spend a week in a private home, you know how trying it can be. There is often little privacy for prayer, study, or rest. Your host and hostess think they must entertain you. Worse still, they think they must feed you! Unless you are in a rural area where public housing is limited, don't put a guest speaker in a private home.

And don't schedule him to eat three meals a day in three different homes! Ask him in advance what his preferences are. He is your guest, not your slave. Many evangelists prefer not to eat a heavy meal before a service; they would rather eat after the meeting. It is foolish for you to force your guest to eat in many homes, because you will simply be curtailing his ministry.

There is debate about this, but it is generally agreed that the parsonage is not the best place for a guest speaker. If the pastor is doing his work during the day (and there is no reason why he shouldn't be working harder), this leaves the evangelist alone with the pastor's wife. Or, it leaves him to babysit with the little children! It takes little imagination to see what can result from such situations.

Give the speaker his expenses and honorarium *as soon as the meeting closes.* This idea of "our treasurer isn't here tonight, so we'll mail you the check" is simply dead wrong. "The labourer is worthy of his hire" (Lk 10:7), and James 5:4 has something to say about holding back wages that are due. *Make sure the check is ready!* Most evangelists depend on offerings for their daily needs, and not all offerings are generous. To make him wait for his money is wrong.

Select the speaker who can best meet the needs of the church *at that time.* Often a fellow pastor from another city will do a better job than some well-known preacher. Some missionaries, home on furlough, have had fantastic ministries in local churches. Don't think that you must choose from a small list of "great men." The Holy Spirit will direct you to the right man.

Should you go after some "great preacher" for a meeting? It depends. Most of the well-known preachers are scheduled two and three years in advance. They simply have to work this way if they are going to use their time wisely in the churches and in the conferences they attend. If you feel led to write a busy preacher, *explain the whole situation to him* — the size of the work, the opportunities in the field, the needs of the church, the financial arrangements, et cetera — and let him make the decisions. If he suggests a shorter meeting, or a meeting at an "off time," don't feel offended. Often a smaller church can have a great meeting with a well-known preacher who comes for a brief time. You can well understand that an effective evangelist or Bible teacher has more opportunities than he can use, and that his desire is to reach as many as possible. If he is a spiritual man, and God wants him in your church, he will get the message. You are better off having such a man in for one or two nights, than to complain because he will not come for two weeks.

As you continue in the ministry, you will learn that different men have different likes and dislikes; and you will adjust to them. You don't treat each child in your family in exactly the same way, and neither should you deal with guest speakers in the same way. Each one is unique, and you must learn to work with them. Don't complain about their weaknesses (we all have them); rather, capitalize on their strengths. If a man's ministry is different from yours, so much the better: the church will hear your message in a new way, and who knows what the results may be?

To what extent should I fellowship with the other pastors in my area? What if a pastor belongs to a denomination that is not true to the Word of God?

The word *fellowship* means "to have in common"; and you certainly have little in common with an unsaved preacher. However, this does not mean you should treat him like an enemy. It is possible to be friendly with him and even help him better understand the Word, but you would not want to compromise your testimony in any way. Kindness is always in order, even when you disagree.

If you limit your friendship and fellowship to the group to which you belong, you may die of loneliness and you may rob yourself of enrichment from saved men of other groups. If a pastor is born again and seeks to serve Christ, regardless of what his denominational ties may be, you can fellowship with him. In fact, he may need you more than you need him. Just about every major denomination today has its evangelicals and its liberals, and we are better off judging (in the best sense) the man himself than judging the man by what he belongs to.

Before we conclude that our own group is pure, let's remember that there was a Judas among the Twelve, and even Peter did not know Judas was of the devil (Jn 6:66-71).

And before we reject those who don't belong to our special group, let's read Christ's admonition in Mark 9:38-41. We may think that our local church is the only true church in town, but in Revelation 2 and 3, Jesus called groups *churches* that had some serious flaws and weaknesses in them!

It has been our experience that we need the fellowship of other pastors. The pastorate is a difficult work, and God's servants can help to hold one another's arms up as we fight the battle together. We recognize the fact that there is a vast difference between acquaintanceship, friendship, and fellowship; and that having a cup of coffee with a pastor friend is not quite the same as asking him to preach in your pulpit. You will find men in your area who may not agree with you on every detail of theology, but whose fellowship will enrich your life and ministry. Get to know them; pray for them; pray *with* them. Major on the important facets of the faith, not the minor things. Learn to listen and you will learn from them.

Even where churches may not be able to cooperate, pastors can still be friends. The unsaved people in our communities enjoy nothing better than a war between pastors. Some pastors, sad to say, thrive on such activities, and even build their crowds by attacking other men publicly. We should certainly defend the faith, but let's make the focus of attention *doctrines,* not *people.* And, pastors have a way of moving on!

What guidelines should I use for building and working with a church staff?

As a church grows, the pastor needs more help. Usually the first staff member to be added is a full-time secretary; then an assistant pastor. Ask God to give you a secretary right out of your church family if possible. If one is not available, perhaps a sister church in the area has a dedicated woman who will do the job.

As you add staff members, be sure to spell out in detail in writing: the responsibilities, the benefits, to whom the worker is accountable, and the financial arrangements. Be sure to be businesslike in these beginnings, because they will set the pace for staff additions in future years. Get started right!

The three basic factors in leadership are: responsibility, accountability, and privilege. Every staff member must be accountable to somebody else; usually this person is the pastor. If you do not balance responsibility with privilege, you may break a man. Too much privilege means no work is being done; too much responsibility means the worker is getting frustrated. There must be balance.

Many pastors find it helpful to meet with their staff first thing Monday morning. The previous Lord's Day is fresh in their minds, and they can share what they have picked up. Go over the week's schedule; make sure there are no conflicts. Update the sick, shut-in, and hospital lists; and assign calls. An hour or so spent with your staff at the beginning of the week will save you hours of extra work later in the week.

Have definite regulations for the staff: lunch hours, coffee breaks, expense accounts, and so on. All of these should be approved by the necessary official boards of the church. In other words, run the staff and the office just the way it would be run if it were a business office and not a church office. "Let all things be done decently and in order."

Don't add too many staff members at one time. It takes time for the church family to assimilate new leadership. A *staff-run* church can turn into a *staff-ruined* church if the members are left out. You don't want the church to get the idea that they pay the workers and watch them do the work!

You should spend time personally with staff members and give them opportunity to share their problems and plans.

Don't permit the church's ministry to become problem-centered. It must be purpose-centered. Their problems are only opportunities for you to see God at work. It is good for staff members to hand in weekly reports of their ministry. This helps to keep the staff up-to-date on each other's activities.

As you add staff members, or replace them, beware of assigning jobs. Job descriptions are helpful, but they are not the last word. In the ministry, we match gifts to opportunities and needs. For example, each youth pastor will have a different approach with the young people: one will use sports, another music, and so on. To expect each man to do exactly the same thing is to embalm the program. You can never duplicate men, but you can discover gifts and give opportunity for their use. The pastor's task is to create the kind of challenge and atmosphere that will make it easy and exciting for his staff to use their gifts.

One of the hardest things a pastor must do is deal with a staff member who is not doing the job. We would like to postpone such a meeting, but we dare not, for his sake and for the church's sake. "Faithful are the wounds of a friend" (Pr 27:6). You must pastor your staff as well as the members of the church. If you have a set schedule for meeting with the staff members individually, you can bring the matter up. If not, you must ask to see him at an opportune time. It will be painful at first, but then God will go to work and you two can face the problem and start finding a solution. Never permit your close personal relationship with a staff member to blind you to his needs.

There are burdens that a pastor who has a growing staff carries that the pastor working alone does not bear. For one thing, it takes time to work with a staff; and time is a precious commodity in the ministry. Ideally, the time you invest in your staff enables all of you to get more work done. If this is not the case, something is wrong. A worker's value is indicated by the amount of supervision he requires. If you must do all his thinking, he is of no value to you.

Another burden is the problem of developing staff faithfulness on the job. It is easy for a church staff to become one big happy family so that time is wasted on long lunch hours, coffee breaks, office chitchat, and so on. We must constantly remind our staff members that they are working for the Lord, and that the Lord expects them to be as faithful in the use of their time as if they worked for some factory and punched a clock. Set a definite time for all of you to be in the office in the morning. You must set the example. We owe it to the Lord and to our people (whose sacrificial gifts pay our salaries) to be faithful and to work hard.

Many pastors get a real hang-up because they usually work harder than their staff. Ideally, a staff member exists so that the pastor can get more done; but this is not always true practically. Just about the time you need him, he is not there! (Of course, the opposite would be worse — a staff member who works harder than the pastor!) Don't get critical; you do not always know the effective ways your staff members are ministering. If you feel you cannot trust them, then you owe them a frank admission of your concern. But don't expect young, beginning assistants to have the same sense of urgency and concern that you have. Occasionally, there are exceptions; but, for the most part, our assistants will never discover the full scope of the work, unless they go out on their own. If we have built into them the basics of the ministry, they will make it.

One final word: there is a difference between delegating responsibility and passing the buck. Staff members resent it when a pastor shoves over onto them the disagreeable tasks he does not want to do. We must be fair with them. When we delegate responsibility, we are giving a man a chance to use his gifts. We keep in touch; we encourage; we provide the backstop when there are problems. Passing the buck means getting something out of our way and forgetting about it!

13

DEALING WITH PROBLEM PEOPLE

How do I go about getting rid of "cranks" and other time-wasters that seem to gravitate to our churches?

Someone has said, "Where the light shines the brightest, the bugs come flying in." It is sad, but true, that a strong Bible ministry will often attract "cranks" and other varieties of strange people, especially in a city church. Here are a few practical suggestions.

Be kind and loving, but be honest and firm. Treat them like Christians, but speak the truth in love. Let them know you appreciate them, but that you cannot devote your whole attention to them. Ask them to pray for you and greet them when you see them. See in them their good qualities and not necessarily their bad ones.

Often these people will descend upon you after a service when you want to talk to visitors or people who were touched by the Word. Here is where godly deacons and elders come in. Have two or three of your good men and women standing near you, and let them rescue you when the conversation gets too long. He says, "Pastor, I hate to interrupt you, but a lady here has a spiritual problem. Perhaps I could chat with Mr. Jones while you help her." This can be done graciously without embarrassing anyone.

These people often have real needs, so seek to minister to

their needs; but never permit them (or anybody else) to monopolize your time. Introduce them to strong members who know how to handle such cases. You never can tell what your ministry of kindness will mean to them in their lonely hours.

Sometimes people will approach you after a service, asking you to endorse some book or product, or explain some long difficult passage in the Bible. Suggest that they phone you during the week, or make a definite appointment right then and there. Explain that the church does not endorse products and that the official board handles such matters. But keep in mind that these seemingly out-of-place requests may really be a cover-up for a deeper need. The person wants to approach you but does not have the courage to do it openly. Some of your greatest opportunities for ministry may be found in situations that, to you, seem out of place. No doubt when Jesus was on earth, He was approached by all kinds of problem people; and we have every reason to believe that He received them kindly and sought to meet their needs. We should do likewise.

Every church seems to have its "chronic critic" and its "boss." How do I go about handling them?

If the church is growing, these problem people may soon be lost in the crowd. They are "big frogs" as long as the puddle is small and shallow. Deepen the waters and they may drown. All of which means: don't focus your attention on the problem people. Focus it on building the church. If you see only the two or three critics when you stand up to preach, your ministry will become sour and defensive. Feed the people. As the body grows, it will better be able to fight off the germs.

When the situation calls for it, face the critic lovingly and honestly. Don't wait for a crisis. Ask God to give you wisdom, and you will know just when to deal with the issue privately. Most critics and "church dictators" cannot face facts honestly in Christian love, so your openness will disarm them. Christ's instructions in Matthew 18:15-20 must be kept in mind. We would hope that these cases would not develop into matters for discipline, but be prepared just the same.

Often the church critic is a person who has been wounded and the wound has never been allowed to heal. Perhaps he was hurt by a former pastor, and now he defends himself from further hurt by criticizing the new pastor. Or, he may be bossed at home, or on the job, so he uses the church as a means of building his own ego. These people have personality problems as well as spiritual problems, and you must handle them carefully. Perhaps God will use your preaching to put them on the road to recovery. Above all else, pray for them.

It does not hurt a pastor to have a critic in the field. It helps to keep him on his toes; it encourages him to do a better job. If all men speak well of us, we may backslide and become self-sufficient.

The "church boss" is as old as the church itself. John wrote about Diotrephes "who loveth to have the preeminence among them" (3 Jn 9). Usually the good people of the church are glad to have a pastor who will handle the "boss" in a sane scriptural manner. It may take a few months, or even years, before he will challenge your leadership; but if you have been ministering in the Spirit, you will be able to operate from a position of strength and authority. Be firm. Be loving. And don't be afraid! Better to face the battle and win than to keep avoiding it and develop ulcers.

Handle this matter the way you plan to handle all such matters, and the message will get around.

How should I handle anonymous letters and phone calls?

Ignore them.

Always look at the signature on a letter first. If there is none, hand the letter to your secretary or a trusted associate, and have him read it. If there is anything in the letter you should know, he can tell you. If you read every anonymous letter that comes, you will get agitated; and Satan will use this to hurt your ministry. People who can help you in your work will not hide. People who love you and trust you will talk to you personally, even if they disagree with you.

Phone calls are a bit more difficult. If you have a secretary, she can screen them by saying, "May I ask who is calling?" If the person refuses to tell, your secretary can inform you, and you can take the call or refuse it as you feel led. The great problem here is this: often needy people will phone a pastor for help, but they want to remain anonymous. This is especially true in large metropolitan areas. If you take the call, ask "What can I do to help you?" and seek to determine whether the caller is a crank, a critic, or a needy case. If he is either of the first two, simply say, "Well, I'm afraid I can't help you" and hang up as soon as possible. If the person is really in need, stay on the line and try to help. Seek to establish confidence so you can suggest a personal conference. More than one desperate person has been saved from suicide by a pastor who took time to listen, love, and pray.

If you have no secretary, you must do your own screening. Experience helps here; so does firmness. Never get agitated; never argue; never carry on long meaningless conversations. Thank the person for calling, suggest that you pray with them right over the phone, and when you say "Amen" — hang up. Above all else, don't carry the conversation around with you and get so uptight nobody can live with you! That is exactly what Satan wants. Commit it to the Lord and go back to your work.

What should I do when people leave the church

"in a huff"? Should I try to win them back, or be thankful they are gone?

Nobody should ever be forced to stay in a church, or be bribed to come back. Matthew 18:15-17 certainly applies here. If something that you said or did caused them to leave, go to them privately to try to straighten it out. If they refuse, take two or three spiritual men with you for another visit. If they still refuse to talk it over and settle it, take it to the church and let the whole body settle it.

Church members who "leave in a huff" are usually saying, like little children in a baseball game, "If I can't run things my way, I'll take my bat and ball and go home." They really believe that their absence is going to wreck the church — and they probably hope that it will! No doubt they have done the same thing in three or four other churches in town. It is unfortunate that we have such carnal Christians in our churches, but we do, and we must face them honestly but lovingly.

Don't encourage them to come back. Don't make concessions. If you do, they will pull the same stunt the next time you rub them the wrong way. Very likely the spiritual people in the church will stand right with you in the matter because they are sick of seeing their church run and ruined by such immature members. If you are new in the church, your spiritual men can clue you in on the background.

Always be kind to these people; otherwise you will add ammunition to their crusade. When you see them, greet them and be kind; but don't give the impression you are anxious to win them back. Pray for them. Don't talk about them except in official board meetings; otherwise the church gossips will add fuel to the fire. You may live to see the day when God will really deal with them and bring them to a place of spiritual usefulness.

Some churches have an "escape clause" in their constitution

that helps to take care of situations like this. It says: "After becoming a member of this church, if we find something that we disagree with either in the doctrine or practice of the church, we promise to ask to have our names removed from the roll." This permits disgruntled people to remove themselves, and also saves you all the problems of further investigation and possible discipline. This clause is not a substitute for church discipline; rather, it is an attempt to obey Romans 12:18 — "If it be possible, as much as lieth in you, live peaceably with all men." By the way, this request for removing their names from the church roll must be in writing.

How do you go about breaking up church cliques?

Be sure it is a clique and not simply a group of good friends who love each other. You want your church members to know, love, and enjoy each other. It is when a group of members isolates itself from the rest of the church and seeks to become a power bloc that you have a clique on your hands.

Cliques are formed in several ways. Sometimes there is a strong member who just naturally attracts people and influences them. This goes to his head and he starts to throw weight around. Or, there may be a problem in the church that needs solving, and people start to take sides. Some of these problems have long histories, and families have a way of taking sides in a definite pattern.

If you feel you have cliques in your church, immerse yourself in Paul's letter to the Philippians. Note how the apostle loved them all ("you all" is a key phrase in the letter) and tried to get them all to love Chirst and one another. He himself set the example in humility and patience. Don't take sides (unless there is a matter of definite policy or doctrine involved), and don't preach at your people from the safety of the pulpit. Be a peacemaker: pray for them all, love them all, and watch for opportunities to pull down walls and start building bridges. Always find something good to say about all who are involved. Keep the bigger issues before the people — winning the lost, sending out missionaries, building the church for which Jesus died. Let the Spirit of God show them their own pettiness.

It often takes a crisis to melt people's hearts. Sometimes it is the pastor who must suffer. No matter: our Saviour suffered for us, and we are privileged to share in the fellowship of His sufferings. Wait — watch — pray — love — and preach the Word positively. God will work and you will have the joy of seeing progress. Perhaps the whole problem may not be solved during your ministry, but you will have helped the next pastor solve it.

There are some churches, unfortunately, that have built-in divisions that seemingly no pastor has been able to remove. We know of one church where an entire Sunday school class refused to accept the new pastor, and went right on functioning by itself, totally apart from the rest of the church! The wise pastor learns to smile at such attitudes, love all the people, and seek to be a blessing to them all. You cannot force people to like you, but they cannot force you to hate them. You can pray for them and ask God to make them what they ought to be. Don't allow the smallness of the few to rob you of the love of the many. Just as the human body sometimes has to function in spite of a weakness or injury, so the spiritual body must function even though it suffers from broken bones. (By the way, the word *restore* in Galatians 6:1 means "to set a broken bone.") If you have to live with such a division, accept it and do the best you can.

One of our members has some peculiar views about Scripture, and he "nails" every new member to convert him to his views. How should I handle this?

Go to him personally and lovingly, after you have formed a good relationship with him. If his views are definitely unscriptural — and this depends on your church's statement of faith — then try to instruct him (2 Ti 2:23-26). His problem may be ignorance, so be patient. If he is definitely holding to unscriptural teachings, and refuses to repent, you will have to take whatever official action is necessary (Ro 16:17-20).

The Bible word *heretic* (Titus 3:10) carries with it the meaning of "one who makes a choice." That is, the man in the church who wants others to make a choice for him or against him is a heretic and is dividing the church. Titus 3:9-11 tells us what to do with him. He should be warned twice, and the third time he should be officially dismissed from the church.

For some reason, just about every church has a member who digs deep into the Word and comes up with unusual doctrines that nobody has ever heard of before. His only way to get attention is to propagate these "important truths." They become his personal test for orthodoxy and spirituality. Instead of using his time to win the lost or edify the saints, he tries to win converts to his cause, not unlike the cultists. In some cases, these members are harmless and the church smiles at them and ignores them. In other cases they become real problems and must be dealt with. Let the man know you love him but disagree with him. Talk to him in private. Try to reason with him. If he will not listen, then you have no other alternative but to protect the church by disciplining him.

14

MEMBERSHIP

**How does a church maintain an honest member-
ship roll? To say we have three hundred members
when we can't find half of them is, to me, deceitful.
I don't want a lot of "dead wood" on the roll, but
neither do I want to use the "hatchet" approach and
hurt a lot of people.**

One way to handle it is simply to put in your constitution:
"Every six months, the pastor and deacons shall go over the
church roll. Any member who has not attended for six months
shall *automatically* be put on an inactive roll. If he returns
and begins to attend faithfully, he shall then be put back on
the active roll." This requirement for active membership
should be explained to all new members, and their acceptance
of membership is proof of their agreement. Nobody should
join the church with his eyes closed!

The church gives this privilege of reviewing the church roll
to the pastor and deacons. This means the pastor does not
have to read the names publicly and embarrass everybody.
It also means that the delinquent member is not "kicked out of
the church" but is simply put into a different category. If
he goes to another church and asks for a letter, the letter
states: "On July 5, 1972, by order of the deacons, Mr. John
Jones was placed on the inactive roll." Again, we must emphasize that this policy must be explained to every new member
so he understands it.

How do you notify the member of his change in status? Actually, pastor and deacons (and Sunday school teachers) ought to be tracking down careless members all year long! A personal visit is in order, if you know where the member lives. (So often the delinquent member is someone who moves away and leaves no forwarding address. In this case, he has no excuse.) Remind him of his spiritual need and that in a few weeks he could lose his full membership. Basically, of course, it is a spiritual problem, and the member needs spiritual help. Be patient — be kind — be prayerful.

It is usually very unwise to send these members letters. A letter is a cold, impersonal thing (unless it is a love letter!); and if it is received at a time when the member is upset, it can do damage. Furthermore. if the member is out of fellowship with the Lord, he could carry the letter all over town and use it to hurt the church. He deserves a visit — and that should not be the last visit. Keep in touch with him; you never can tell what God may do for him.

All of this demands personal concern and attention on the part of pastor and leaders, *but it is worth it.* We are members of the body of Christ, and as such, we must minister to each other. The church that cares is the church that grows.

It may take a few years for you to get such an arrangement in your church program, so be patient. When your members realize that such a policy does not slam the door on members, nor does it embarrass people, they will readily accept it. Church membership should be a valuable, meaningful thing; and this is one way to accomplish it.

How does a pastor go about building church loyalty? There are so many extra-church organizations these days competing for the time, money, and energy of my good members, that I hardly know what to do.

Feed your sheep and love them. God will give you spiritual ties that will be stronger than any ties another organization can manufacture. Don't go around criticizing other groups; many of them are being used by God in wonderful ways. In fact, if all our churches were busy doing what God wants done, many of these groups would never have been organized.

The biggest mistake many pastors make is *failing to involve their people.* Mature Christians with talents and spiritual gifts want to go to work. If the local church does not use them, some other group will. The growing edge of your local church is the new convert: *put him to work.* Of course, he is not ready yet to teach a class or serve as deacon, but he can go visiting and start sharing his faith. He can work in various ways in the church and use his abilities for the Lord. In most cases, the new Christian is just bubbling over with energy, and that energy must be directed into challenging ministries.

There are, sad to say, some church members who prefer to work in extra-church organizations for reasons that we would consider less than Christian. There is more prestige, for one thing. In the local church, we try not to put people on pedestals. Furthermore, there is usually more freedom and less discipline in an outside organization. "Whiz kids" who get frustrated by church policies and procedures escape to outside organizations where they can do what they please. You can be thankful if they are not a part of your official family.

On the other hand, there are many fine, loyal church members who feel it is God's will for them to serve in other organizations. These people will be loyal to you and to the church, but they may not always be present at meetings. Their ministry will take them elsewhere. Fine! Perhaps they are doing more good sharing Christ in another church than sitting listening to you. Don't be upset; learn to cooperate with the inevitable.

Get to know the leaders of these extrachurch organizations.

Some of them might even be a blessing to you! Don't be afraid to disagree with them, but do it in the right spirit.

In your ministry, emphasize to your people the importance of the local church. (It is interesting that these extrachurch organizations that often criticize the church go to the church for their support!) Organizations come and go, rise and fall, but the local church goes right on. Its work might not be as exciting as that of some other group, but in the long run, it may be more lasting. As your own ministry of the Word blesses the people, they will come because they are being fed. Keep the church program moving; plan ahead; keep them involved. Let them know often that you love and appreciate them. In time, their hearts will be knit together, and they will love their church and support it.

How much time should I spend with fringe members who really don't support the church or my ministry? Shouldn't I spend more time with the faithful members who are doing the job?

Ephesians 4:7-16 teaches that the pastor's task is to equip the saints to do the work of the ministry. You cannot equip people who are outside the influence of your ministry. We would emphasize winning the lost and equipping the saints: this is what builds the church.

This does not mean that you ignore the fringe members. Get to know them, visit them on occasion, pray for them. One day God will give you a real opportunity to get through to them, and you will be glad you kept the door open.

We cannot prove this statistically, but it seems that there are three groups in every church. Let us assume that the top ten percent are going to be spiritual if there is no pastor — these are the pillars of the church; the bottom ten percent would not serve God if the apostle Paul were their pastor; the middle eighty percent or so will go one way or the other.

Now, if you invest time in the top ten percent, they can reach down and pull up the eighty percent! (This is Ephesians 4 in practice.) And as the eighty percent start to move, they will touch that lower ten percent. In other words, it may be that some of your members can do a better job encouraging the fringe crowd than the pastor can. Fine — let them do it!

Please don't spend all your time trying to rescue the few. And don't permit them to rob you of precious time that belongs to the faithful. The healthy sheep reproduce after their kind: keep them healthy!

At what age should children be permitted to join the church?

In churches of the Reformed tradition, children become communicant members at baptism and then are received into full membership at confirmation. The procedure varies from group to group and even from church to church. We will discuss the problem as it relates to the churches that receive their members on profession of faith. (Of course, *any* prospective member ought to be able to give a personal testimony of his faith in Christ, regardless of what the membership procedure may be.)

The issue is not so much *age* as *maturity,* and "child differeth from child in maturity." As children are not all the same size at the same age, so they do not all have the same spiritual perception at the same age. To receive a child who is too young to know what it is all about is to rob that child of a better spiritual experience at a later time. Anyone who has ever worked with teenagers knows the recurring problem: "I was supposed to have been saved when I was six, but now I'm not so sure."

Too often, Christian parents push their youngsters into decisions, and in later years the children rebel. Every pastor has heard the plea of the doting mother: "Oh, please take Junior

in! You should hear him pray at the table! We just know
God is going to make a missionary out of him!" Too often
in later years, Junior becomes a mission field instead of a
missionary.

Our counsel would be: take each individual separately and
be sure there is some kind of evidence of spiritual life and
growth. Obviously, a child's expression of his faith is not
going to be identical to that of an adult. If it is, beware of
imitation. If the child is truly born again, to postpone baptism
and church membership a few years is not going to destroy
his soul. Following the biblical pattern of the Jews, many
churches set twelve as the minimum age for membership; and
this seems a good idea. Children who grow up in Christian
homes often show signs of spiritual life earlier; but, again,
we want to warn against imitation, or decisions made simply
to please the parents. It would be wise to have sixteen as
the age for full voting privileges in the church. It is doubtful
whether a twelve-year-old member could vote with much in-
telligence or spiritual discernment.

How can we best assimilate new converts and new members into the church family?

Present them to the church publicly so that everybody has
the opportunity to meet them. Some churches use a new members' reception. Encourage officers to invite the new members
into their homes. You and your staff should set the example
here.

Use the buddy system (or the Timothy system) and relate
the new member to another good member of the church.
They can go calling together, for one thing. New converts
are the growing edge of the church — use them!

It is unwise to thrust new people suddenly into places of
responsibility, but do use their talents and gifts as soon as

possible. Going to work for the Lord is the best way to feel at home in a church.

These things should not be left to chance. You, or someone on your staff or among your officers, should carefully direct this ministry, led by the Spirit. A new member with the wrong church friends could become a problem!

15

CHURCH DISCIPLINE

If a church officer has been caught in some serious sin, and he confesses it and makes things right, should he give up his office? If so, how soon can he come back again to serve?

We know of no place in the New Testament where church officers are put on probation after making things right with God and their church. Peter confessed his sin and was immediately restored to fellowship and service.

However, two factors must be considered: his own spiritual life, and any loss of confidence on the part of his fellow church officers. When we confess our sins, God immediately forgives; but sometimes there must be a period of recuperation before we are strong enough to serve. And, if the other officers have doubts, it might be wise to suggest a furlough. This does not mean the officers reject the confession; rather, it means they have too great a love for the offender to let him hurt himself by beginning to carry his spiritual responsibilities too soon.

Above all else, *keep these matters private.* The greater the place of responsibility, the greater the damage when the leader sins. There will be some cases when the wisest move is for the offender to resign quietly after making things right. If his confession is sincere, he will not balk at this suggestion.

133

What is church discipline and how do we practice it? How can we get it started in churches that have ignored it?

Discipline is an important part of the Christian life. God disciplines His children (Heb 12), and we must discipline ourselves (1 Co 9:24-27). God expects the pastor to discipline his children (1 Ti 3:4-5), and also to discipline the church. Church discipline is actually God exercising spiritual authority through a local church for the purposes of reclaiming an erring believer and maintaining the purity of the local church.

Church discipline is *not* a pastor "throwing his weight around," or a church board acting like a police court. Church discipline must be God at work in the life of the church, or it will not succeed at all. Matthew 18 describes the necessary ingredients for successful discipline: humility (1-6), honesty, (15-18), obedience to the Word (18-19), prayer (20), and a forgiving spirit (21-35). Unless a church has the right spiritual atmosphere, discipline will do more harm than good. Before you can even begin to start practicing it, you must get your church into the right spiritual condition, and this takes time, prayer, love, and spiritual preaching.

If you believe in church discipline, then talk the matter over with the pulpit committee *before* accepting the church. In as loving a manner as possible, let the church know that you want to obey the Word in this matter. Explain that discipline is not an evidence of hatred, but of love. If you love your members, you will want to rescue them from sin. 1 Corinthians 5 indicates that discipline is for the good of the offender (1-5), the good of the church (6-8), and even the good of the unsaved society that needs our witness (9-13).

Who should handle discipline? It begins with a concerned pastor (Heb 13:17, 1 Pe 5:1-4). 1 Timothy 5 advises that we pastors treat our people like members of the family: the older members as fathers and mothers, the younger as broth-

ers and sisters (vv. 1-2). We advise the pastor to take the
first steps, and not to involve the official board or anybody
else. Of course, most churches have procedures laid down
either in the denomination's book of discipline or the constitution; but these principles should not prevent the pastor from
privately meeting with a suspected offender and seeking to help
him. It has been our experience that offenders are relieved
when the pastor, in love, talks to them privately, man to man,
friend to friend.

Of course, if our private interview does not help, then
Galatians 6:1-3 comes into play: take some spiritual men with
you. Jesus says the same thing in Matthew 18. If this does
not work, then the whole church (unfortunately) must be
involved (see 1 Co 5). When sin is not confessed, it has a
way of growing and involving more people.

Here are a few guidelines to follow:

1. Before you make any serious accusations, be sure you have
   witnesses (1 Ti 5:19, 2 Co 13:1).
2. If the case is especially serious or the offender hostile,
   take a witness with you when you make that first contact.
3. Try to be impartial (1 Ti 5:21).
4. Don't jump the gun! Read Proverbs 18:13, 17 and 1
   Timothy 5:22. Take time to pray, think, and wait;
   but don't permit caution to keep you from acting.
5. Don't expect to be aware of everything! (1 Ti 5:24-25).

As we see them, the cases requiring church discipline are
as follows:

1. *Personal difference between two members* (Matthew 18:
   15-18; Philippians 4:1-3). Don't pry into personal feuds
   until at least one member has tried to obey Christ's instructions.
2. *Refusal to work* (2 Th 3:6-16; 1 Ti 5:8).
3. *Doctrinal error.* We begin with patient teaching (2 Ti 2:
   23-26). If this fails, we use rebuke (Titus 1:10-14 and
   Gal 2:14). The final step is avoiding the person (Ro 16:

17-18) and rejecting him from the fellowship (2 Ti 2: 18 and 2 Jn 9-11). We advise you to be careful with people who have doctrinal problems. There is a difference between ignorance of the Word and deliberate false teaching.

4. *Repeated troublemaking* (Titus 3:10). The member who goes around the church membership asking, "Are you on my side or the preacher's side?" should be given two warnings; the third time he "strikes out." He should be dismissed from the fellowship if he persists in causing divisions.

5. *Open sin* (1 Co 5, Gal 6:1-3). The attitude of the church must be that of mourning that such a thing should even happen in the fellowship. The offender is given opportunity to repent and make matters right. If he refuses, he must be dismissed. (The Greek word means "expel, drive out.") This is the official act of the majority of the church. Of course, if he repents, he can and should be forgiven and received back (2 Co 2:6-11).

Some church members think discipline causes trouble, but this is true only if it is carried out in the wrong attitude. Loving discipline in a church always unites the family, just as it does in a home. It strengthens the authority of the Word; it honors Christ; it challenges the church to new levels of spiritual experience. It also strengthens the testimony of the church to outsiders. Who pays any attention to a church where anything goes?

Remember the principle: private sin, private confession; public sin, public confession. Never hang dirty wash out in public. It is not necessary to explain the sordid details to the whole church, especially with children and teenagers present. If a person comes forward for reinstatement, let the church know that you and the officers have dealt with the matter, and that the person should be forgiven and received. This can be a precious experience of forgiveness and love!

Like medicine, the best kind of discipline is preventive. The Word, when faithfully preached, exercises discipline. Keep your eyes open for beginnings. God gives His shepherds a "spiritual radar" that helps them detect the beginnings of sin; and at that point, we must act. Pray for God's direction, and He will give you opportunity to speak to the person at the right time. If you handle discipline in the right way, it will make your people love you more, because they know you care too much to permit them to sin. "Faithful are the wounds of a friend."

Finally, it is worth noting that you do not use a cannon to kill a flea. 2 Thessalonians 3:6-16 suggests degrees of discipline: exhorting (v. 12), holding aloof from (vv. 6, 14), and publicly warning the person (v. 15). "Not as an enemy, but . . . as a brother" is wise counsel. Final public expulsion is the last resort, and we would trust that the offender would come to his senses before that is necessary. But, if it is necessary, don't be afraid to act. Just be sure your men are with you, and obey the Word in the spirit of meekness.

Sometimes discipline — or backsliding, at least — hits the pastor's own family. If a member of my family goes wrong, must I leave the ministry? If so, what work is open to me?

What our children do after they leave home is not always under our direct control. We believe that if children are raised right, they will be inclined to live right; but more than one Christian worker has had a son or daughter turn prodigal. And, praise God, many of these prodigals eventually find their way back home!

We see no reason why a faithful pastor should leave the ministry because a member of the family has gone wrong. Why have *two* victims? Do church officers step aside when their children go wrong? Not usually.

We must confess, however, that a man's ministry can be hurt by the poor testimony of a family member. This may be a burden he will just have to live with. If he finds this really cripples his work, then he ought to move to a new sphere of ministry. Life isn't over yet: God isn't finished with us.

Often it is not the church members who are hardest on the pastor: it is his fellow pastors! Brethren, let's be loving and forgiving. Matthew 7 is still in the Bible. Christian love forbids us to record here the names of some great men of God whose children have broken their hearts: the whole matter is in God's hands. For that matter, many a servant of God has seen a new touch of God on his ministry because of the heart-ache of a family crisis. We are not suggesting that we "do evil that good may come of it," but rather that God is able to "turn the curse into a blessing" (Neh 13:2).

16

THE PASTOR AND HIS HOME

To what extent does my wife share in my ministry?

In one sense, since "two become one," she shares in it as much as you do. The pastor who cannot confide in his wife and let her help share the load is destined for a lonely ministry. Our homes often say more to our people than do our sermons. A pastor's home ought to be a quiet benediction to the neighborhood and community and to the church that he serves. The home is primarily the responsibility of the pastor's wife, and it is here she must give herself in ministry, particularly when the children are small.

How much actual activity she shares depends on the woman herself. Some women are quiet and retiring and do their best work behind the scenes, training and encouraging others. Other women joyfully accept places of leadership and service in public. Your wife must be herself and not an imitation of someone else. When you move to a new pastorate, give your wife time to get the home settled and functioning smoothly before you ask her to take church responsibilities. Another woman can teach the "Sunshine Class," but no other woman can be your wife or the mother of your children! Put first things first.

Neither the pastor nor his wife should become so indispensable that their departure would make the church's ministry collapse. Help your wife develop the female leadership in the church. One very fruitful field of service is with the newly married women, helping them get started right as wives and, eventually, as mothers. Often the pastor's wife assists her husband at weddings, and this is a natural contact with the young brides. However, she should also have a ministry among the other women of the church as a friend, confidante, and encourager.

The important thing is that your wife know herself, be herself, and fulfill the ministry God has given her. Some members of the church may want to pour her into a mold, but you resist it. Your individual ministries will blend and be a blessing when both of you are serving as God has planned. When you find yourself tense and frustrated, then one or both of you must make a change. As you pray together daily, God will guide you. It is an exciting thing to grow together as husband and wife, serving together in His work!

This leads to another question: Is it wise for a man to pastor if he is not married?

Matthew 19:12 indicates that a man's marital status may stem from more than one cause. A man must determine God's will for his own life. Better to live in single loneliness than married "cussedness."

But, all things considered, it is wise for a man to seek a wife in the will of God. Many good men have pastored successfully without being married: Clarence Macartney and Robert Murray McCheyne come to mind. But there is something about the Christian home that enriches the pastor and the church. The qualifications in 1 Timothy 3 do not demand marriage, but they do assume it. The present unrest in the Roman Catholic church concerning celibacy is an indication that something is lacking.

Many of the problems a pastor must face in counseling have

to do with marriage and the home. True, he can study and observe and perhaps become an expert in marital relations. But somehow, our people have in the back of their minds, "Yes, but he's never been through it!" It is one thing to speak from authorities and quite another to speak with authority, the kind of authority that comes from wholesome personal experience.

Don't make the quest for a wife the central thing in life. Be the kind of a Christian man you ought to be, and God will do the rest. When the right one comes alone, you will be glad you waited.

To what extent is the pastor's home a part of the ministry?

The pastor's home is a part of his ministry, but it should not be a part of the church building. He and his family should have as much privacy as any other members of the church Where the pastor is unfortunate enough to have to live near the church, he should not allow members to stop in before church or hang around after the service. It may take a few misunderstandings before he gets the point across, but it must be done. No pastor's wife can stand being a hostess seven days a week.

Your wife is the "mistress of the manse," the "princess of the pastorium." Never make plans for the use of your home without consulting her, unless you want to lose your happy home. Women are sensitive about matters that men never will understand, and a spiritual wife is only too happy to cooperate if she is given the chance.

Certainly we ought to use our homes to the glory of God. "Given to hospitality" is one of the requirements for the ministry (1 Ti 3:2). Peter gives this same commandment to all church members in 1 Peter 4:8-9, so it must be important.

Whom do we entertain and when? Try to have your officers

in at least once a year. (In larger churches, you will have to schedule this throughout the year!) New members appreciate the opportunity of getting to know the pastor better. The youth of the church ought to be included, and invite the college students when they are home for holidays or their summer vacation. Not all of these times need to be full-blown dinners. Snacks after church can mean just as much. Try to have the newly engaged couples over, and the newly married. Give them a living example of a happy Christian home.

Some pastors have found that a 4:00 Sunday afternoon dinner is suitable. The wife usually prepares a special Sunday meal anyway, and there is a terminal point: you all have to go to church. It may make Sunday a bit more of a burden for your wife, but it has the advantage of saving a week night for both of you!

Be sure your wife keeps a record of who was served and what was served. She should do this with visiting speakers and missionaries as well. A record saves embarrassment, and it also helps her in planning future meals. Knowing what each person likes and dislikes (she will learn quickly enough!) will help make her the ideal hostess.

One of the occupational hazards of being a pastor's wife is the sudden discovery that you must entertain within the hour! What do you do? You plan ahead! Having the makings of a tasty dinner or dessert on hand has saved many a pastor's wife from ulcers and embarrassment. But you won't have to tell her this: she knows more about it than we do!

How can I be a faithful pastor, husband, and father all at the same time? How can I avoid friction between the home and the church?

Conflicts can best be avoided by being one man and always being yourself. A happy home and a happy church are made up of the same ingredients: love, discipline, sacrifice, the Word, and prayer. We should be as loving in the church as we are at home, and we should be as disciplined at home as we are at the church. It is when a man separates home life from church life that he gets into trouble. The pastor must be one man, and not two. He does not "change hats" or attitudes when he leaves home and goes to the church, unless he is pretending in one place or the other.

The pastor ministers to his family when he ministers at the church. He ministers to the church when he ministers at home, for a successful Christian home is the greatest strength of the local church. We are *always* pastors, *always* husbands, *always* fathers. To say we are not or to act as though we are not is to court a nervous breakdown and ulcers.

A pastor must spend time with the family. Dr. Henry Brandt reminds us that it is not the *quantity* of time, but the *quality* of time, that counts. You deserve a day off, and you cannot spend every evening in a committee meeting. Fortunately, most pastors can arrange their own schedules and budget their time. Often it means sacrifice, but life is made up of sacrifices.

If you and your wife are in accord, the children will not suffer. If your wife is upset because of the schedule, you had better take time for an inventory. If any one of the children begins to show signs of problems because of the schedule, stop immediately and get some professional counsel. Each child is different, and some children demand more attention than others. It is not necessary to sacrifice a child for the success of a church: God can take care of both.

Your own personal devotional life, and your times of prayer with your wife, are keys to success in this area. The two of you set the atmosphere in the home. Keep alert for signals that tell you it is time for a change in family plans.

How can a younger pastor protect himself from designing women in a church?

Age has nothing to do with it! Many a mature pastor has fallen in this way, and "let him that thinketh he standeth take heed, lest he fall."

If your own marriage is all it ought to be, no woman on earth can tempt you. We defeat germs by maintaining good health, and we deal with this particular sin by maintaining a healthy marriage relationship. If you find yourself thinking seriously about any other woman, you had better head for home and start repairing the damage that has already been done there. Your wife may not always tell you, but there are definite SOS signals that a husband who cares will not ignore.

Pay attention to your wife in public without being demonstrative. Let others know you love her; be a gentleman, no matter what the other men might do. Designing women rarely move in unless they sense there is a chance for success. Let them know there is nothing they can cling to.

Watch out for the perpetual female "counselee" who has to see you after every service. Suggest she talk to your wife or that you and your wife together counsel with her. If she refuses, you have discovered the truth. Often your wife will detect the kind of person she is before you see it, so respect her views. Also, beware of the woman who phones for help just about the same time every month. This is often a signal that there is serious emotional trouble. She and her husband may be having trouble, and both may need professional help.

It is unwise to counsel women when you are alone. Your church office should be adjacent to that of a secretary, or an assistant, if possible. If you must go to the home, take your wife or a trusted officer along. If she *insists* on absolute privacy, arrange for it in a place where there is a lot of glass and some people on the other side!

Don't permit the single ladies in the church to form a fan club. It is difficult to have a spiritual ministry among people who see you as a substitute husband or boy friend. You do them very little good, and they do you a great deal of **harm**.

1 Timothy 5:1-3 suggests that we treat the members of the church as we do the members of our own family. This is wise counsel.

A pastor does not have to commit an immoral act to ruin his testimony and ministry: he just needs to be *suspected.* The loose tongues will take care of the rest! "Keep thyself pure." The fact that *several* women hang around you is no assurance of safety. One pastor warned his handsome assistant about the women, and the boy said, "But there is safety in numbers." "Yes," said the pastor, "but there is more safety in exodus!" Joseph would have agreed with that advice.

We repeat: if your own marriage is all it ought to be, you will have no problems along this line. Watch and pray!

17

PERSONAL MATTERS

How should I budget my time so I will accomplish more each day?

An efficient day begins with an effective quiet time before the day begins. Jesus arose early in the morning to pray (Mk 1:35, and see Is 50:4-5), and certainly we cannot do less. It was John Henry Jowett who said that he had to be at his desk working when he heard the workmen's boots sounding on the street, for how could the servant of the God lie in bed while the members of his flock were already at work? (*The Preacher: His Life and Work*, p. 116). Unless you begin your day in the Word and prayer, committing the entire day to Him, you will not make the best use of your time.

Use your mornings for study and be in your study at the same hour each day. Don't make a public announcement that you want to be left alone unless you have the kind of rapport with your people that can stand a strain. Their attitude is (right or wrong): "We pay his salary, and he should be available!" It takes time, but gradually educate your people not to phone or stop in ("I was in the neighborhood — ") when you are preparing their spiritual meals. A word in the ears of your best officers may help get the message out.

Devote your afternoons to visiting, mail, phone calls, and church administration. Make all your necessary phone calls at one time and they will go faster. When you read your mail, jot down replies in the margins and you won't have to read the letters again when you reply. Try to set up counseling appointments for afternoons as much as possible. No doubt your evenings will be given to necessary committee work, visitation, and those important times at home with your own family.

Learn to say "no!" to outside invitations, especially during your first year or two. A pastor does need to get out but not to the neglect of his flock. Add responsibilities and ministries gradually, and never take on a new ministry until you feel at home with the ones you already have. Too many men feel they must set the world on fire their first month on the field. They start publishing a paper; they begin a daily radio ministry; and they feel obligated to speak at every meeting in town. Their branches go our farther than their roots go deep, and eventually the tree falls over. There is nothing wrong with church publications and radio programs, or with speaking at other meetings; but these things must come *in their time.*

Carry a pocket secretary and use it. Don't trust your memory; don't write yourself notes on little pieces of paper. Carry the kind of memo book that gives you space to write: appointments, jobs to be done, expenses, and special notes. *Use it!* Arrange a schedule for the day, the week, and the month. Each evening, check off the jobs completed and make a new list for the next day. All of this sounds very elementary, *but it works!* This is the program followed by the masters of industry and by men and women who get things done.

Make a list of the jobs you are doing and see how many of them can be done by others. This is not passing the buck. It is *delegating.* There is no reason why the pastor has to run the mimeograph machine, fold the bulletins, lick the stamps, and mend the hymnals. There are people in the church who can do these jobs better than he can. After all, the pastor's task is to help the members do "the work of the ministry" (Eph 4:11-12).

There will be days when your schedule will fall apart, but you need not fall apart with it. Roll with the punches and trust God to help you get your work done. Have definite priorities. Put your preaching first (next to the cultivation of your spiritual life). Your church will rise or fall on the strength of your pulpit ministry.

Take a day off each week, and take your alotted vacation. "But the devil doesn't take a day off!" True, but the devil does not have a physical body. And Satan is hardly our example in the ministry! Jesus knew that His disciples needed a time of rest (Mk 6:30-32), and He knows that we need rest, too. Pick the day that best suits your "body clock" and church schedule. Monday is not always the best day: you often hear of things on Sunday that ought to be taken care of immediately, and there goes your day off. Thursday is a good break, especially after working up to a midweek service. And don't overdo it on Saturdays. Many great preachers of the past would not be out on a Saturday evening, but would spend that time preparing their own souls for the Lord's Day and praying for their people.

Finally, never waste odd minutes. If you are going to the barber shop or the doctor's office, take a book along and avoid the five-year-old magazines. As suggested in Chapter 6, you should plan to relax a bit before and after your evening meal and use that time to read. (This practice is also good for digestion.) That is a good time to work your way through your magazines.

During the day, if you find yourself getting nervous and tense, stop to pray and turn everything over to God. The Holy Spirit is infinitely efficient; He alone can lubricate the machinery of your life. It is when we trust in our own strength and wisdom that we go on time-wasting detours. "Let the peace of God [be umpire] in your hearts" (Col 3:15).

How can I maintain a burden for souls, and communicate this burden to my people?

As with visitation, soul-winning is better caught than taught. If the pastor has a burden for souls, it will show up in every aspect of his ministry — preaching, teaching, administration, counseling, weddings, funerals, et cetera. Soul-winning is not something we turn on and off like the radio. It is the central concern of our lives as we seek to glorify Christ.

We maintain our burden for souls by doing the job. The more we share Christ with others, the brighter the fire burns. When we feel our hearts getting cold, we must pray for the Spirit's fullness and then go out to win souls! We must ask God to make real to us what it really means for a soul to be lost and without hope. If we are in daily fellowship with Christ, our hearts will be kept warm and tender.

Read books about great soul-winners and about evangelism. You cannot read a life of D. L. Moody, Billy Sunday, or Gipsy Smith without your own heart being moved. This does not mean we live on "borrowed fire," but it does mean we seek inspiration from their lives. Even soul-winners who are now in heaven can provoke us unto good works!

Have a list of lost people and use it for regular prayer and visitation. When you meet with your officers for prayer, share the names of the unsaved. As these people come to Christ, it will bring great joy to your heart and to the hearts of your leaders. Nothing fans the sparks of zeal like the joy of seeing souls come to Christ.

What should I do when I hit one of those discouraging days in my ministry?

The first step toward defeating the blues is this: *expect to have dark days.* All the books on the deeper life notwithstanding, you will have days of discouragement and defeat.

Moses had them; so did Elijah, David, and Paul. (Have you read 2 Corinthians 1 lately?) Don't feel you have lost your calling or sinned away God's blessing just because you have a cloudy day.

When that day comes, face it honestly. It does no good to put on an act. Above all else, *make no important decisions!* Many a good man has hurt himself by resigning out of the will of God, simply because he felt he had failed.

Talk it over with a close friend, and pray for God's grace. Spend some time with your wife and the children. Get out and get ventilated! Sometimes the basic cause is physical: what you need is fresh air, exercise, and a change of pace. (Remember Elijah?) When you feel one of these dark days about to hit you, make your plans accordingly.

Be patient with yourself and with the Lord. "This too shall pass." It is amazing how different the situation will look twenty-four hours later! Watch out for self-pity: this is the poison that kills the ministry. Also, beware of getting critical of your people. Everything looks out of proportion at night, so wait for the sun to shine. When God gives you light, you will see that most of the things you feared were really only shadows.

In many cases, simply committing yourself to God and going out to minister to somebody else will start you on the road to recovery. There is no therapy more potent than trying to encourage another child of God. If you sit at home sulking, or sit in your study licking your wounds, you will only get worse. Do something active! Before long, the old confidence and joy will come back.

Pastors who suffer from chronic discouragement, even to the point of despair, should secure professional counsel.

How often should I minister away from my own field?

The first year you are on a field, you must stay close to home. You need to be in the pulpit, feeding the flock, and giving them opportunity to get to know you. After that, you can think about a wider ministry.

If you are sensible and put your church first, the people will let you make your own schedule and will not complain. If you are away too much, you will only hurt yourself and the church. If you find yourself *wanting* to be gone, perhaps it is time you considered a change. A spiritual father loves his children in the Lord and he wants to be with them. The sheep need a steady shepherd, not a kangaroo who hops in and out of the pasture. If while you are on the field, you faithfully minister to the people, they will not begrudge you opportunities to minister in other places. In fact, they will be proud that their pastor is in demand.

Of course, a church needs to be taught that the pastor's wider ministry is good both for him and for them. It is good for him in that he has a change of location and pace, and is able to be a blessing to others. It has been our experience that the wider ministry is more difficult than staying at home! But we invariably return home anxious to minister to our people and having learned something new and fresh while away. It is good for the church when the pastor is away occasionally. They get to hear other men, and they get a blessing by sharing their pastor with others. After all, the pastor is a gift to *the* church as well as to *a* church (Eph 4:8-15).

Except for his annual vacation, or other special occasions, the pastor should not be away two Sundays in a row. When he finds himself a stranger in his own pulpit, he is gone too much! If he detects that the sheep are restless, then he had better stay home and get his job done. Baby-sitters are fun, but they can never raise the family. Some churches have a set number of weeks for the pastor to use for outside meetings. If so, abide by the policy and don't complain. If God wants

to give you a wider ministry, He will also give opportunity for
making necessary changes in the policy. Just be sure that, when
you go elsewhere to preach, you do so because you want
to be a blessing, and not because you want to escape your own
church!

Finally, keep a close watch on the total church calendar,
and don't be away at important times of the year. Your
church is your *base* ministry, not your *sphere* of ministry;
but don't undermine the base! If you do, you may find you
have no ministry at all.

**I'm embarrassed to ask this, but here goes: how
do you go about letting a church know you need a
raise? Is it unspiritual to discuss finances with the
church?**

Most churches have a policy of reviewing salaries annually.
A pastor ought to get at least a cost-of-living increase, and,
if the work of the church is prospering, he deserves a merit
increase. Discuss this with the board before you come to the
church and find out what their policy is. You owe it to them
(and to your family) to be open and direct, without seem-
ing to be grasping.

One thing you must never do is bring your personal finances
into the pulpit, or drop hints here and there in the church.
Your wife especially must be careful not to discuss money with
the other ladies in the church. Talk to God about your needs,
and be patient. If the church is insensitive to your needs, God
will meet the needs some other way and the church will be
the loser. It is unfortunate that some churches try to get
bargains when they call a pastor, and they wonder why God
never seems to bless them. The church that takes care of its
pastor will discover that God will take care of the church.

There is always a need for total stewardship education in

a church. If you are preaching the Word faithfully, you have to deal with giving; and don't skirt the issue!

Usually, in every church, the pastor and his family discover one family that becomes very close and precious. Sometimes you can open your heart this way, but only if God opens the door. It is unwise to play one member against another. You could end up raising your salary but lowering the spiritual level of the church.

If a man wants to be rich, the ministry is not the place to go. It has been our experience that God meets every need, that He gives us above and beyond what we deserve, and that any sacrifice made is more than compensated for in other ways. Do not become obsessed with money. Matthew 6:33 is still in the Bible.

How can I make my own devotional life more meaningful?

The pastor handles spiritual treasures day in and day out, and if he is not careful, they will lose their wonder. The man who makes six or eight visits a day, and prays in each home, may find himself praying in a rather routine fashion. Constant study of the Word can become routine. Phillips Brooks in his *Lectures on Preaching* rightly said, "Familiarity does not breed contempt except of contemptible things or in contemptible people." The problem does not lie with the Word or prayer, but with the minister's heart.

Give yourself time to meditate on the Word and pray. Start each day with a definite meeting with God. Once you begin to measure this meeting on the clock, you will start to put out the fire. No matter how busy we may become, we must never permit the morning watch to be neglected.

Many pastors find it helpful to use a different translation for their devotional reading in the Bible. We can become so familiar with the beloved Authorized Version that it no longer speaks to us. A wide margin edition is helpful because you can write notes in the margins as God speaks to you; but be careful that your devotional time does not become a time for sermon preparation! We are meeting with God to hear Him speak to us — to our needs — and if He meets our needs, He will work through us to meet the needs of others.

Use a notebook for a devotional diary. Have separate pages for prayer burdens. If we pray about the same things every day, our prayers can become perfunctory. Write down the truths God gives you as you meditate.

If we are ministering to our people as we ought, there will be sufficient burden on our hearts to make us want to pray and feed on the Word. God has a way of putting us into the furnace when we need it! The closer you come to the needs of people, the less sufficient you will feel yourself to be, and the more you will have to turn to God for help.

Read the great devotional classics, but not as a substitute for your Bible. Many great preachers of the past read a sermon a day just to feed their own souls. Remember, the pastor usually does not get to hear anyone else preach; and his own soul can be starved for a sermon! Don't always read sermons by the same preacher, no matter how much you enjoy him; but vary the spiritual diet.

Occasionally meet with a fellow pastor for a good season of prayer. Fortunate is the pastor who has a praying friend. Be honest with each other: it will do you both good.

Our spiritual life starts to deteriorate when we start praying things that we don't mean, preaching things we don't practice, and expecting things of others that we don't do ourselves. It is important that we take time to examine our own hearts for any signs of erosion. We must apply the Word to our own lives before we dare apply it to the lives of others.

No doubt you will discover certain parts of the Bible, and certain devotional books, that will just hit the spot when battle fatigue sets in. Get off to yourself, away from home or church, and let God clean the old ashes from off the altar of your soul.

You cannot separate the inner life from the outer life. One of the best ways to stir up the flame of devotion is to go out to minister to somebody in need, or to win a soul to Christ. "Give and it shall be given unto you." A self-centered devotional life is not a Christ-centered one. We receive the living water that we might be a channel to share it with others (Jn 7:37-39).

Where can a pastor take his troubles? My wife and I talk things over, and I pray a lot; but I often wish I could just unload on some saintly apostle or prophet!

The loneliness of leadership is one of the most difficult things to bear. If you read biographies at all, you know this is true.

Psalm 23:1 can be translated, "The Lord is my Pastor." We believe that God wants to pastor His undershepherds, and that He is able to take us through the difficult places of life. Certainly there is special grace for the man who preaches the Word and shepherds the flock.

But it is also good to have someone to share our burdens with, and this is where the older, more experienced pastor comes in. Fortunate is that young man who has a mature pastor-friend to whom he can go with his problems. It is unfortunate that too many "successful preachers" have been inaccessible. Perhaps they must be if they are to get their work done. But usually in every area there are godly men whose doors and hearts are open to their younger brethren. Even a telephone conversation over the miles can help lift the burden.

Sometimes you will find a godly couple in the church whose hearts seem bound to your heart, and you can feel free to talk with them. It is unwise to open your heart to just any-body in the church, but the younger pastor can share his bur-dens with some mature couple (or perhaps an older officer) and not have to worry about the consequences.

Above all else, *beware of self-pity!* Self-pity is the first step to defeat in the ministry. If you find it invading your heart, *get out and do something!* Loneliness and self-pity often travel together. Play golf, go for a walk, or take your wife window-shopping — but *do something!*

Does the Lord ever lead a man to resign when he has no other place to go?

Not usually. We find very few, if any, men in the Bible just standing around waiting for God to direct them. One task is usually the preparation for the next. In fact, not having a church could be a serious barrier to getting a church! Most pulpit committees are looking for a man who is busy in a church and doing something.

It has been our experience that God begins to stir the heart long before He moves the body. If you are walking with the Lord, He will direct you and His timing will never be off. Many pastors resign in haste and repent in leisure. Had they only waited a few months, the tide would have turned and the work would have prospered. Dr. V. Raymond Edman, for many years president of Wheaton College, often reminded the students, "It is always too soon to quit."

The lives of Bible men, and the lives of great men of the church, all seem to indicate that God works patiently, accord-ing to a definite plan. God rarely keeps a man waiting and wondering.

18

THE PASTOR AND HIS PRIORITIES

What are the real priorities in the ministry?

1. *Your own personal devotional life.* Everything you do rises or falls on this. "Without me, ye can do nothing."

2. *Your family's faith.* Our ministry begins at home. Another man can pastor the church, but only you can be father and husband in your home.

3. *A burden for souls.* Keep the fire burning! Otherwise your ministry becomes cold and academic.

4. *Study.* Don't settle for secondhand sermons: do your own work and dig for the blessings. Guard your morning hours and invest them in concentrated study.

5. *Preaching.* History reveals that the achievements of the churches rise or fall depending on the preaching of the Word.

6. *Pastoring.* This personal contact with your people will balance the work for you. The preacher must be a pastor if the Word is to touch lives in a personal way.

We don't look upon priorities as rungs on a ladder, but rather as spokes in a wheel. The hub of the wheel is your walk with God: everything else comes out from that. Paul did many things, but they were all controlled by that decisive "this one thing I do!"

How does one measure success in the ministry?

It is odd but true, that most of the successful pastors in history felt themselves to be failures. Perhaps it is because a growing man is never satisfied with where he is: he wants to reach higher to the glory of God.

If the pastor is growing personally, then the church will be growing. If there is a sameness and tameness about your life, watch out! If there is no excitement in the study of the Word and the preparing of messages; if pastoral work is boring; if you find yourself arriving at the office late and leaving early; if you discover you are defensive; then spiritual erosion has set in, and both you and your church are in danger. If the work is a challenge, and if you eagerly anticipate ministering the Word publicly and from house to house, then it is likely that God is blessing and the work is growing.

There is a book in the Bible called Numbers — but numbers are not everything. Where there is life, there is growth. Spurgeon used to say that the only preachers who criticized statistics were those who had none to report! Perhaps he was right. The Holy Spirit counted numbers in the book of Acts, but the numbers were the results of the ministry of dedicated men and women. We want our churches to grow, not so that we can count people, but because people count. Sometimes there is a slow, steady growth; at other times, God gives rich harvest. But numerical increase is one indication that God is at work, provided the increase is not the result of man-made, carnal gimmicks.

Increase in offerings is also a test of spiritual success. If the sheep are fed, they will give. When they are starving, they start biting each other!

When your ministry is being blessed of God, there is an atmosphere of love, confidence, and service in the church. For the most part, the people will love each other and seek to minister to each other. You will always have problems, because a church is made up of people; but these problems will not be crises that threaten to sink the ship. The ability of a church to face and solve problems is an indication of spiritual growth. Also, the appearance of *new* problems indicates that you are going somewhere. Never be afraid of disagreements in the church: where there is movement, there is friction. The lack of friction may mean the church is no longer on the move!

If you have set definite goals for your ministry, the achieving of these goals will be an indication that you are making progress. The pastor who simply drifts from week to week will always be discouraged, because he does not know for sure where he is going.

2 Corinthians 10:7-13 is a clear warning against the wrong kind of self-evaluation. It is easy for a church to become a mutual admiration society. The true measure of a church's ministry is not what it is doing as compared to some other church (which may be smaller!), but what it is doing as compared with *its own potential.* The church that could have a thousand in Sunday school, but rests content with two hundred, is a failure.

Never forget that churches go through stages of growth, not unlike that of the human body. The "babyhood" stage of a new church is exciting — just like having a baby in the house! But then things settle down, and you reach a "childhood" stage when the church must be taught and trained. There is an "adolescent" stage when your people seem to manufacture problems! Once you reach a place of spiritual maturity, *keep it there!* Be sure that the church is winning souls so that new life is coming into the body regularly. Once a church gets into that stage of spiritual "old age," you will have serious problems. The next step is "second childhood" (Heb 5:12)! It is a wise pastor who senses the times and the seasons, and who preaches and plans accordingly.

One word of encouragement: the Lord rarely lets a pastor

see how much good he is doing. When you feel the most discouraged, God is probably using you in the greatest way. Be faithful. God will take care of the rest (1 Co 4:2).

Moody Press, a ministry of the Moody Bible Institute, is designed for education, evangelization and edification. If we may assist you in knowing more about Christ and the Christian life, please write us without obligation to: Moody Press, c/o MLM, Chicago, Illinois 60610.